AIR
RACING
TODAY

AIR RACING TODAY

THE HEAVY IRON AT RENO

Philip Handleman

MBI Publishing Company

To Cleveland,
a place of great spirit
and happy memories.

This edition first published in 2001 by MBI Publishing Company
729 Prospect Avenue, PO Box 1, Osceola, WI 54020-0001 USA

© 2001 Philip Handleman

Previously published by Airlife Publishing Ltd, Shrewsbury,
England

MBI Publishing Company books are also available at discounts in
bulk quantity for industrial or sales-promotional use. For details
write to Special Sales Manager at Motorbooks International
Wholesalers & Distributors 729 Prospect Avenue, PO Box 1,
Osceola, WI 54020-0001 USA.

Library of Congress Cataloging-in-Publication Data Available.

ISBN 0-7603-1117-X

Printed in China

Author's Note

All of this book's photographs of air racers and air-show aircraft, their pilots and ground crew, are not posed but candid shots. I have attempted to capture aviation aspects of the Reno air races as they occur each September in the high desert of Nevada well north of the casino district. The focus is on the Unlimited Class and AT-6 Class racers, what air-racing aficionados affectionately call the 'heavy iron'. These aircraft, the biggest, the loudest, and, in the case of the unlimiteds, the fastest, attract the largest followings each year at the Reno air races.

The photographs incorporated here are mainly of activities at the Reno air races in 2000. However, in an effort to provide the greatest spectrum of color and aircraft types in modern air racing, a sprinkling of scenes from other years dating back no further than 1995 can be found as well. There are also a couple of images from the old Phoenix 500 air races, which illustrate a brief discussion of that once promising but ultimately ill-fated venue.

Acknowledgements

The event known as the Reno air races enjoys a world-class reputation as a successful showcase of air racing and flying displays. This well-deserved stature derives from at least a couple of factors.

First, the event's leadership has been dedicated to maintaining the pre-eminence of the world's longest-running air races. For many years, Thornton Audrain managed the Reno air races. His shoes are now being filled by Michael Houghton, whose official title is President of the Reno Air Racing Association (RARA), which oversees the National Championship Air Races (NCAR). A lean executive board provides general direction, while a larger group, known as the air race directors, addresses specific concerns such as concessions, parking, security, etc. Wisely, Reno/Stead Airport manager Skip Polak serves as one of the air race directors.

Second, the organization's 2,500 volunteers have been absolutely indispensable to not only making the Reno air races happen, but in helping the event to thrive and to serve as a model for other aviation events. Each of these wonderful people contributes to making the Reno air races an inescapably entertaining experience. From the photographer's perspective, the invaluable interface with the volunteer corps comes repeatedly throughout each day of the races, starting before the first contest in the early morning, when a briskness usually marks the air. The thoroughly independent-minded members of the Washoe Search and Rescue Squadron, a loosely knit coterie that one might refer to as a Jeep brigade, provide reliable and avuncular escort to the waiting pylons.

Although physically far removed from the air-racing site, my friends at Airlife Publishing Limited, publishing director Anne Walker and marketing director Andrew Johnston, remain continually supportive of my mission to record airplanes in words and pictures. Managing editor Peter Coles thankfully continues to offer his sage counsel and apply his steady hand in ways that enhance the end product. Also on these projects, the towering presence of the late Alastair Simpson, a gifted and benevolent leader at Airlife and within publishing circles generally, has often been felt. Many books ago, he offered encouragement and demonstrated his belief in me, for which I am eternally grateful.

Most of all, my thanks go to my wife, Mary. Whether, in any given year, she accompanies me to the Reno air races or tends to important matters back home, her spirit is always with me, by my side and in my heart. In the infrequent interludes of quiet out at the pylons I think of her, knowing that she, in turn, is thinking of me. After the 2000 Reno air races, when we were in the clutches of a cold autumnal spell in our native Michigan, we decided to brave the chilliness, bundle up in our leather jackets, and launch into a radiant, Reno-like sky. Aloft in our Stearman, communicating with each other over the headsets wrapped in our cloth helmets, we marveled together at the natural beauty, the splendor, the glory only men and women of the air can behold. And then, I told myself how lucky I am to have Mary to share this passion for flight.

Contents

Introduction

Few, if any, human endeavors match the unexpurgated thrill, the cascading rush of air racing featuring the souped-up heavy hulks of World War II vintage. I have always felt privileged to witness these exciting vignettes in the history of aviation from the rarefied vantage point of the pylons that mark the course for the contestants.

If there is, as hypothesized, something endemic in human nature that causes humankind to seek newer worlds, to go faster, farther, higher, etc., then surely the once-a-year air racing activities at Reno qualify as a key manifestation of the phenomenon. For here, in dramatic fashion over the vast desert floor, humans are pushing the proverbial envelope ever closer to the edge, reaching, stretching, grasping for an ounce of more power, an inch of extra space, a spurt of additional speed. It is more than a race; it is akin to an expedition, an exploration, or a search for limits.

Yes, there are excesses of self-promotion – what in today's lexicon is referred to simply as hype. Then, too, there is the obligatory machismo. But out at the pylons, where the flying is happening and the only visible participatory components are the sky, the desert, and the aircraft, one experiences the singular sensation of the planes coming on and then, in a maddening flash, whizzing by in a dazzling blur, leaving behind gut-wrenching reverberations.

With each turn of a pylon, there is a quest for something new and better, a striving to get ahead. Strange as it may seem, out here in the middle of a desert where wind storms kick up the surface sand, the human species is imperfectly, indeed haphazardly, elevating its place in the world. This circling of pylons at breakneck speeds in its own improbable way is an ennobling pursuit, an inspiring spectacle. I try to be as close as possible to the confluence of the forces at work, to the core of the inspiration, as near to the pylons as prudence permits. Each time the air racers approach, turn, and then speed away, I laugh inside with unrestrained joy, purging accumulated inhibitions in the presence of unvarnished boldness.

I have often thought that the unique perspective of the races as viewed from the pylons and the inner rewards that flow therefrom offer an opportunity to transform troubled or distracted children. Would it be possible, I have wondered while riding the crowded media bus across the show line onto the sandy trails to the pylons to photograph the races, to squeeze in a couple of children from disadvantaged backgrounds? Perhaps, with a little encouragement under a mentor's wing and the memorable, inherently inspiring sights and sounds of thundering air racers as hardly anyone else gets to witness them, it would make all the difference in the world. Boys and girls otherwise set on a dead-end course might catch the dream of flight and soar to great heights. The magic of the Reno air races makes you believe that possibilities are infinite.

CHAPTER 1

The Wondrous World of Air Racing

Halcyon Days: Cleveland

Cleveland, that unassuming industrial city tucked into the heartland of America, for its contributions to air racing during the exciting Golden Age of Flight, will always touch a sympathetic chord in discussions of the great sport. Spectators numbering in the hundreds of thousands gathered almost every Labor Day weekend through the 1930s at the city's municipal airport to witness aviation's coming of age. On this grassy flatland, aeronautical dreamers turned bold concepts into dynamic realities. Futuristic configurations scribbled on restaurant napkins took shape as bumblebee-shaped aircraft poised to challenge existing speed records.

The ascendancy of Cleveland came naturally. Less than two decades before the start of the National Air Races the brothers who promulgated modern aeronautics, the ingenious Wilbur and Orville Wright, experimented on the open expanse of a sparse cattle ranch nestled in Ohio's quaint countryside. Here, near Dayton, just where the Midwest's recumbent landscape begins ever so gently to spout waves of rising terrain, at its conjunction with the less convivial mountains of the Border States, the aeronautical value of the wide open spaces was realized. In a logical progression, the military established a flight school and an avia-

One of the many pylons marking the course for air races at Reno, Nevada shines in the stillness of early morning. In the distant sky, another marker of sorts – a full moon – garnishes the curtain of blue. (*2000*)

tion research unit near the grounds where the Wrights refined their earliest powered flying machine.

The Army installations, under various names – first McCook, then Wright, and eventually Wright-Patterson – became a hotbed of flying activity, the testing of new systems and airframes being important priorities, especially as the U.S. edged closer to involvement in World War II. Advanced configurations, capable of speeds and altitudes unthinkable only a short time before, were honed at Dayton and sent half a world away to win the fight for democracy.

The ennobling sphere of flight testing flowered in the years succeeding the war. The ineffable Chuck Yeager, then a young captain having achieved ace status in the European theater, came to this outpost in Ohio, a kind of clearinghouse and nerve center for his legendary flights in rakish-looking X-planes over the Mojave Desert. Although the first sonic boom generated by a manned plane was heard out West, the achievement had much of its origin in a part of the Midwest that has come to be referred to as the cradle of aviation. Today, the gangling control tower of Wright-Patterson Air Force Base looms on the horizon as one looks out from amid the overgrown brush of hallowed Huffman Prairie, this surprisingly sculptural symbol of cutting-edge technology standing in poignant juxtaposition to the unadorned field that accommodated the first fledgling airplanes.

Where Dayton, in the southwest section of Ohio, provided the impetus and developmental foundation for flight, Cleveland, in the northeast corner, offered the industrial wherewithal and public fascination. Raw materials, shipped via the Great Lakes, passed through a thriving maritime terminus. Copious quantities of iron ore, funneled into teeming plants, were transfigured into rock-hard steel that could be used for wheel brakes or engine parts. Machinists operated huge presses that formed metal sheets that might become wing spars or cabane struts. Tools were devised and fabricated to assemble airplanes on mass production lines, enabling the construction of vast numbers in a fashion not unlike the methods used to manufacture automobiles.

Whatever the factory requirements, it seemed that resourceful Cleveland could produce the necessary equipment. One of the city's more forward-thinking businesses, Thompson Products, saw the future in aviation, and sponsored the coveted Thompson Trophy for the fastest pylon racer at the annual National Air Races. Perhaps not coincidentally, the aircraft parts maker, founded by Charles E. Thompson and so closely associated with the classic air races of 1930s Cleveland, is today, through a combination of internal growth and astute mergers, the aerospace powerhouse known as TRW. Cognizant of its roots, the company continues to make its home in Cleveland.

A shining light of the races no less bright than the revered Jimmy Doolittle captured the Thompson Trophy in 1932 by shepherding the ornery Gee Bee around the closed course at Cleveland. In the process, he set a new closed course record with an average speed of 252.7 mph. Roaring to unprecedented speeds in purpose-built designs, the racing pilots of the day, attired in silk scarves and leather helmets, ignited the public's enchantment with flight. These swashbuckling daredevils, the authentic heroes behind the sometimes trite Hollywood characterizations, were the perfect elixir for the national malaise prompted by the Great Depression.

Further acclaim awaited some of the racing pilots. The already famous Doolittle led the historic raid of sixteen B-25 medium bombers on Tokyo from the heaving deck of the *Hornet* aircraft carrier. He received the Medal of Honor, and went on to command the Army's Eighth Air Force in Europe. During World War II, Tony LeVier, a longtime Lockheed test pilot, made the maiden flight of the P-80 Shooting Star, America's first operational jet fighter. Later, in 1955, he made the first flight in the top-secret U-2 spy plane. Steve Wittman, a talented tinkerer, developed efficient designs for the do-it-yourself market. In his later years, he took on a kind of godfather status to the sport aviation movement, and the airport in Oshkosh, Wisconsin, site of the big annual fly-in of the Experimental Aircraft Association, is named in his honor.

The pilot who most personified the drama of the air races, immortalizing them in the public imagination, was the one-and-only Roscoe Turner. A barnstormer in the days following World War I, the highly experienced Turner brought his colorful flying repertoire and his equally colorful personality to Cleveland. His adeptness at enhancing the speed of aircraft designs, integrated with his airmanship skills, made for an unsurpassable juggernaut. He carried away the Thompson Trophy three times, which is more than anyone else. Also, he set the closed-course record for pre-war air racing in 1938.

Always clad in a military-style uniform that he had tailored to his specifications, and usually exhibiting a charming smile, Turner was the ideal subject for newspaper photographers and newsreel cameramen. He projected both a daring and a confidence that drew many people to the world of flight. When finally he settled down, it was as the owner/operator of an aircraft servicing facility in Indianapolis, Indiana. Long after his racing exploits, he continued to advocate forcefully and eloquently the imperative for maintaining a strong aviation industry.

Cleveland's manufacturing prowess and proximity to essential natural resources were duly recognized. With the outbreak of war, the government saw the advantages of having an aeronautical research facility in this bastion of engineering, and in 1942 the National Advisory Committee for Aeronautics established the Lewis Flight Propulsion Laboratory (later the Lewis Research Center and now the Glenn Research Center at Lewis Field) on property adjoining Cleveland's airport. The historic strides in the aeronautical sciences emanating from this research center contributed to the metamorphosis of aviation. In time, aviation would no longer be characterized by haphazard venturing in the backyard shed, but instead evolve into a global enterprise of nearly incalculable influence.

At the onset of the space race in the late 1950s, the newly formed National Aeronautics and Space Administration superseded the old agency and took control of its myriad properties. Over the years, NASA's facility in Cleveland has been tasked with solving many vexing problems, including those related to propulsion systems. The dedication and ingenuity of its researchers, highlighted in Tom Wolfe's book *The Right Stuff*, have opened the way to flight far beyond the atmosphere in vehicles that were the stuff of pulp fiction in the time of the air races in Cleveland.

In contrast to many other states, Ohio, owing in large part to its being the birthplace of aeronautical development, saw extensive airport construction within its borders. In an implicit recognition of the importance of flight, there is even now, as general aviation airports disappear with alarming frequency across the nation, an abundance of airfields dotting Ohio's landscape. This valuable infrastructure, developed over the many years since the Wrights' early successes, combines with the state's generally level terrain to make for an inviting flying environment. Given the factors that beckon one into the sky, it is hardly a surprise that the first American to orbit the earth, John Glenn, and the first human to walk on the moon, Neil Armstrong, began their journeys to the heavens from this alluring panorama in Midwestern America.

From spring through autumn, the mural-like vista of Ohio's remaining patchwork quilt, as viewed from the air, evinces a sense of what it must have been like to fly over the almost totally unblemished countryside in the days of the classic air races. Imagine the raspy whine of a pulsating radial engine piercing the restful turquoise-and-orange sky at twilight, the pilot easing the throttle forward in measured strokes in a test run the day before the official race. Skimming low over the cultivated flatlands, the ground passes in an onrushing blur, the fruits of the fecund soil giving off the pungent fragrance of the unspoiled land, a magnificent and reassuring reminder at each inhalation of its inescapable everlastingness, the platform of every launch and of each return.

Banking hard left at the juncture of a pylon rising starkly from the otherwise uninterrupted space, the pilot hugs the obstruction, trying to minimize his drift away from the course, always equating distance with time – the shorter the interval, the quicker to the finish line. He works his controls, the pressures increasing to where he must apply all the muscle that can be mustered. Tilted at nearly ninety degrees, the wings standing practically upright, the flying wires generate a unique twang as they vibrate incessantly in the turn. The mechanics and lineboys, tinkering with the other racers, crane their necks to catch a glimpse of the demon screeching past no more than a wingspan above the unforgiving ground. In one corner of the field, removed from the busy pit area, a cadre of neighborhood kids, having climbed the fence, peers awestruck at the low-flying racer.

The forces of nature build inexorably, subjecting the cockpit's occupant to the encumbrance of nearly four times his body weight pressing against him. As the magnitude of the accumulated Gs becomes nearly unbearable, wings are leveled and the plane zips down the straightaway, by now a spectacle of astounding speed, a sleekly shaped hulk of metal transformed into an indistinct flash. The aroma of burnt gasoline, before dissipating into the crispness of the coming night, temporarily evidences the plane's torrid flight.

These invigorating scenes came crashing to a precipitous end with the outbreak of World War II. The races were suspended from 1940 through 1945. Upon their resumption in 1946, the technological and developmental revolutions that had occurred in the short span of the war years manifested themselves conspicuously in Cleveland. The racing planes were no longer the one-off creations of entrepreneurs, but the mass-produced combat aircraft of defense contractors. Moreover, the increasingly routine use of the jet engine in the waning days of the war meant that aviation would soon leap to another generation, leaving piston-powered aircraft churning in their wake.

The races, previously infused with enormous anticipation as the

The Reno air races are an action-packed four days, encompassing not only races in a variety of aircraft classes but an ongoing air show. Here, the Canadian military air demonstration team, the Snowbirds, makes a dramatic arrival as unlimited racers are prepped in the pit area. (*1996*)

crowds did not know until the event what the racing planes looked like or whether a new world record would be established, turned into more predictable affairs. The propeller-driven machines had attained their zenith by the end of World War II, and now it would be jets dictating the upper limits of speed. Of course, jets were the exclusive preserve of the military. Even so, performance specifications of the new types were more or less a matter of public knowledge, the exotic-looking silvery fighters having been wrung out during their flight test programs well before any highly touted race.

Interest had already begun to recede in the races when, in 1949, tragedy struck. The incurable post-war phenomenon of urban-suburban sprawl was getting underway, the green zones around many airports, including Cleveland's, being subjected to encroachment by real-estate developers. One of the unlimited racers, a highly modified P-51 Mustang, careened out of control into a nearby home, killing a mother and her child along with the pilot. The disturbing news sent shock waves through the racing community. It looked as if Cleveland's glory days as the pre-eminent air-racing venue were due to be terminated.

If a revolutionary powerplant technology and a horrific fatal accident were not enough to extinguish the races, the tepidness of corporate sponsors and the beginning of hostilities in Korea would cause a certain end. Companies were skittish about associating their names with a sport that seemed no longer to connote technological advancement and suffered from a perception as unsafe. Meanwhile, the military was calling up its reservists for active duty, leaving the roster of racing pilots sparsely filled. Also, the Air Force would not be able to send its usual contingent of demonstration aircraft to the races now that a new war on the other side of the world had to be fought.

After 1949, the air races that had come to represent a kind of September magic no longer graced the skies over Cleveland. The weekends of thrilling aerial competitions were now the stuff of lore, to be passed on by those lucky souls who witnessed the greatest of aviation's pageantry.

Resurrection: Reno

Through the 1950s and the early 1960s, there were no National Air Races. But this did not mean that enthusiasm for the sport waned within the flying community. In fact, during those 'quiet' years, airplane buffs around the country nursed surplus World War II warplanes back to airworthiness. Mustangs, Bearcats, Corsairs, Lightnings, Warhawks, Thunderbolts, and more, purchased for a fraction of their production costs, were saved from the scrap heap by aviation devotees who recognized a hidden value in these old combat aircraft. The restorers knew that these planes had been piloted to victory by typically unheralded young men who comprised a part of that segment of the population now known as 'the greatest generation'.

At austere airstrips scattered across the land, restorers labored almost always individually and anonymously, refurbishing famous aircraft types one at a time. At first, it was just a matter of keeping the old planes flying, seldom an easy task given that the military had worn the equipment hard. After all, these aircraft were made for combat. Gradually, a movement sprang from the diffuse centers of restoration. In places like Texas and Wisconsin, like-minded pilots and mechanics bonded into loosely knit organizations dedicated to preserving the historic warplanes of the recent past.

This was all part of a larger phenomenon taking hold across America. The post-war years saw the birth of the weekend pilot. These flyers were not just the returned military aviators, but average citizens enthralled by the idea of flight and who, because of affordable planes and an accessible airspace system, were taking to the skies in unprecedented numbers. For a while during this post war euphoria it appeared that Henry Ford's vision of an airplane for every family might actually come true. Ford's concept, devised a generation earlier, for a 'flivver' as a means of personal transportation, an aerial version of his Model T, had faded out almost as soon as it had been envisaged. Now, in an ironic turn of events, Piper Cubs and Aeronca Champs rolled off assembly lines and ascended into the sky signaling a new-found popularity for light sport planes. The key, however, was not necessity, as with cars, but sheer joy in the experience.

An infrastructure developed. Small, privately owned commercial airports arose on what were once cow pastures or cornfields. Flight schools sprouted up on these fledgling airstrips. Names like Cessna, Piper, and Beech backed their evolving designs with parts supply networks. The government even got into the arena by installing a nationwide system of radio navigational aids that were compatible with relatively low-cost receivers the private pilots could mount in their instrument panels.

For the first time, aviation was within the reach of almost anyone desiring to partake of the adventure of flight. A solid body of grassroots activists was created. The participants represented a new foundation for aviation. Now, sport flying could be viable as a commonplace occurrence, not merely an extravagance. The growing number of enthusiast organizations, notably Paul Poberezny's Experimental Aircraft Association, held regular flying events aimed at bringing together members of the flying fraternity. These fly-ins offered a means by which pilots could exchange information and showcase their airplanes. The most meticulously restored aircraft at the fly-ins were recognized with the bestowal of an award. Just arriving in an antique was not quite good enough any more. Your peers were out in force, and they would notice an unpainted cowling or frayed interior upholstery.

The most peripatetic of World War II aircraft in the post-war years, the Stearman biplane trainers, many of which were put to commercial use immediately after the war as agricultural applicators, started showing up at fly-ins not in their workaday untidiness. Instead, exuding a personal pride, their owners emblazoned them with stunningly authentic yellow or yellow-and-blue paint schemes that harked back to the time when the aircraft were in military service. Long a favorite of air-show performers, some of the venerable biplanes were decorated in combinations of bright hues like red and white with starburst or checkerboard patterns on the wings and tail surfaces.

Whatever the colors, owners came to care about the appearance of their restored military trainers, establishing a tradition of not hesitating to carry on board a bottle of detergent and wiping away any residue of splattered oil upon arriving at a fly-in. The combat planes from World War II, the fighters and bombers, though far more expensive in every regard, also began to appear by the early 1960s as beautiful re-creations, in some ways even surpassing their wartime effulgence.

Concurrently, air shows became a favorite pastime, a fixture ingrained in American culture almost as deeply as baseball. Indeed, the Air Force and Navy established full-time flying demonstration units, the Thunderbirds and Blue Angels respectively. For its part, the Army set up a team of parachutists known as the Golden Knights. At air bases and civil airports around the nation, people flocked to flying expositions. Military open houses and major air shows in every corner of the country occurred with regularity, allowing the townsfolk to take a peek at immaculately restored antiques and high-performance planes.

In this conducive atmosphere, a handful of insightful men banded together to revive the National Air Races. Only this time, the races would be far removed from Cleveland or any similar metropolis. The catalyst was a prominent rancher and pilot in the desert community of Reno, Nevada. Bill Stead, enamored of flying and an accomplished World War II air combat veteran, had yearned for years to see air racing reborn. Finally, in 1964, Stead and a core group of local civic and business leaders whom he had inspired were able to dovetail their dream of rekindling the National Air Races with the state of Nevada's centennial celebration scheduled for that year. The state, seeking novel ways to promote itself on the occasion of its hundredth anniversary, provided barely enough seed money to the air-race organizers for them to proceed. With a shoestring budget but an abundance of determination, Stead and his hardy band of compatriots fostered the return of air racing, albeit at an inauspicious dirt airstrip on the periphery of Reno known simply as the Sky Ranch.

Conditions at the bare-bones airstrip did not augur well for the future of the sport. The racing aircraft kicked up clouds of dirt, their propellers fanning the brown powder in all directions, caus-

ing eyes to water and hampering visibility. Such a state of affairs made the races untenable for large audiences and even jeopardized their very continuance. The troublesome site was tolerated for one more year after which, serendipitously, a nearby military air base announced its impending closure.

The city took over the base, which, interestingly enough, had been named in memory of Stead's brother, Croston, who had perished in a flying accident while serving with the Nevada Air National Guard. Known now as Reno/Stead Airport, the facility is located ten miles northwest of Reno on a welcome steppe shadowed by imposing mesas. Tragically, Bill Stead also lost his life, in the spring of 1966 piloting a Formula One racer in Florida. Ironically, despite having spawned the revival of the National Air Races, he never got to see their flowering at Reno/Stead Airport, where they have been held every September since 1966.

Nevada, a desert domain noted for its crystalline air and prodi-

For a few years in the mid-1990s, air races were conducted at a second air-racing venue that had been established near Phoenix, Arizona. Known as the Phoenix 500, these races, though no less thrilling than those at Reno, were unable to match the staying power of the longstanding Reno event. After a promising beginning, the Phoenix 500 quietly faded from the scene. (*Phoenix 1995*)

gious land mass, offered an ideal setting for flight in the modern era of fast-moving planes. It is hardly coincidental that the Air Force established its premier fighter weapons school in the wide open spaces of this Western state. Just north of Las Vegas, at Nellis Air Force Base, combat pilots from the air arms of each of the American military services and allied forces from around the world gather to compete in heralded Red Flag exercises. These match-ups mirror real-world air combat scenarios and are geared towards sharpening air fighting skills. In perennially blue skies over tens of thousands of uninhabited acres, jet fighters duel in mock dogfights. Whole air battles are fought in these boxes of specially designated airspace known as the Nellis ranges. In a fascinating manifestation of cutting-edge technology, every nuance of the action in the ranges can be monitored in a master control room at the base. The ranges have been wired with high-tech devices that can decipher the efficacy of the participating aircraft, permitting the controllers, who sit in air-conditioned comfort on the ground, to score each performance. Afterwards, the results are reviewed with the crews so that their flights become highly dissected learning experiences.

Here, too, the Air Force's elite air demonstration squadron, the Thunderbirds, makes its home. For a team that must perform a precise aerial ballet virtually every weekend from March through November, and that in true Air Force tradition is permitted no excuses, Nevada's good year-round flying weather is a major plus. When they are not 'on the road', the Thunderbirds are at home practicing their superb maneuvers, honing their impressive repertoire, reaching for perfection in their flying routine.

If any downside exists to their stationing in this desert climate, it is that on summer afternoons the ambient temperatures on the ramp easily exceed a hundred degrees Fahrenheit. The unsung enlisted personnel, aware of the trade-offs, uncomplainingly tackle the demanding maintenance requirements of the team's F-16s. Oblivious to the inhospitable elements out on the flight line, they do their job, they keep the team's jets in the air.

Farther north, the state turns overtly rugged. And here, the government has long coveted the remote stretches of desolate land. As the Cold War heated up, the Central Intelligence Agency wanted a secure airfield where it could flight-test a new generation of spy planes, starting with the U-2, such that it would have reason-

A fixture at the Reno air races is the legendary Robert R.A. 'Bob' Hoover, one of the greatest air-show pilots of all time. Shown here is his Shrike Commander, a twin-engine corporate transport in which the expert stick-and-rudder aviator has performed exquisitely before millions of admiring fans. Medical and insurance issues grounded Hoover on occasion in the 1990s, but even when not flying he has retained a visible profile at the Reno air races. (*1999*)

able assurance that no one outside the so-called 'black world' would get a glimpse. The Air Force's existing Flight Test Center at Edwards Air Force Base in southern California's Mojave Desert was just too close to Los Angeles to provide the necessary secrecy.

In 1955, the then head of the Lockheed Skunk Works, the irrepressible Clarence 'Kelly' Johnson, who oversaw the design of the U-2, dispatched one of his most trusted test pilots, none other than Tony LeVier of air-racing fame, to scout out possible locations for this super-secret air base. Departing from Lockheed headquarters at the Burbank, California airport in the company's Beechcraft Bonanza, LeVier flew on a diversionary course to make it appear that he was not flying on any special mission. When sufficiently distant from Burbank, he veered in the direction of Nevada and began searching for a suitable site. After scouring the barren landscape, there was really never any question in his mind as to the preferred location once he caught sight of a large, naturally occurring dry lakebed encircled by mountains. The lakebed would make a perfect landing strip and the craggy terrain around it would act as a wall to deter curiosity seekers.

The airfield-to-be was known as Groom Lake, and, as luck would have it, this Godforsaken place already fell under the purview of the federal government. Both the Air Force and the Atomic Energy Commission (now the Department of Energy) had already recognized the intrinsic value of this spot's remoteness. It was depicted on U.S. Geological Survey maps that divided huge swaths of the Nevada desert into numbered sections. Most of the dry lakebed fell within the section labeled Area 51.

This simple, unembellished description – Area 51 – would, in time, take on a significance of oversized proportions as it came to represent the most stringently classified of U.S. military weapons programs. By the 1980s and through the early 1990s, sightseers came from afar to peer from adjoining cliffs, trying to steal a glance at the super-secret aircraft that allegedly operated there. With the intrusions turning into a cottage industry, the Air Force finally clamped down, closing off the sole remaining look-out point.

A small subculture of science-fiction zealots has even claimed that aliens from other planets, along with their flying saucers, are housed at this outpost. Almost every unexplained aerial sighting is attributed by these cult-like characters to the goings-on at Area 51. Hollywood, noting the obsession, not surprisingly jumped on

The dominant racer in the Formula One Class for nine straight years was *Nemesis*, a state-of-the-art racer designed, built, and piloted by the talented Jon Sharp, an engineer at the fabled Lockheed Martin Skunk Works in Palmdale, California. This racer, incorporating every aeronautical advantage imaginable and permitted under the rules, won every race in its class from 1991 to 1999, after which it was donated to the Smithsonian Institution's National Air and Space Museum. Sharp, in his specially tailored flight suit, is seen riding with crew as his unique racing plane is towed to the starting point on the ramp. (*1997*)

the bandwagon with pure exploitative ardor. Television shows and motion pictures with a sci-fi bent have not hesitated in recent years to portray Area 51 as a top-secret installation shrouded in layers of mystery, suggestive of governmentally inspired conspiratorial mischief.

The truth is that soon after LeVier's overflight, he and his boss, Kelly Johnson, landed on the lakebed with a picnic lunch. Walking the hardened surface, kicking spent shell casings along the way which had lain there since the lakebed's use as a gunnery range years before, Johnson decided this secluded tract of land fitted the need for a secret base where his futuristic military designs could be validated. Surmounting substantial logistical hurdles, Groom Lake was quickly made into an air base.

Over the years that followed, a succession of once unimaginable aircraft, including the high-altitude U-2 spy plane, the Mach 3 SR-71 Blackbird, and the F-117A stealth fighter, alighted into the sky for the first time from this remote hideaway in the vast desert of Nevada. At all times, security has been uppermost in the base's operation. Heavily armed guards patrol the perimeter in all-road vehicles and helicopters. Signs warn that deadly force will be used to stop intruders. In fact, the isolated base was so secret that the Air Force would not publicly acknowledge its existence until legally forced to do so in the 1990s in connection with court proceedings.

One can hardly help but speculate about the hybrid and prototype aircraft that have possibly rolled down the runways at Groom Lake. The Tacit Blue technology demonstrator, a bathtub-shaped test platform created to verify low-radar cross-section concepts for the Northrop Grumman B-2 stealth bomber, probably operated from this covert site. Also, there were claims that the much-rumored Aurora hypersonic reconnaissance plane flew out of Groom Lake in a natural progression following its earlier Lockheed Skunk Works stable-mates. Known by nicknames like 'Dreamland' or 'Paradise Ranch', this enigmatic airstrip hidden away in Nevada's capacious desert has become a lasting part of aviation's mystique.

Continuing north within the sprawling Nellis ranges, one comes to the auxiliary base at Tonopah, which, like Groom Lake, is set in the middle of nowhere, a place for anonymity to be savored. Here, Air Force pilots are known to have flown surreptitiously obtained Russian fighters, learning the strengths and weaknesses of the potentially adversarial aircraft. Also, the first operational stealth fighter unit, the 37th Tactical Fighter Wing, was based at Tonopah. Because of the need for secrecy, all aircraft were flown only at night and pilots were shuttled back to Nellis by chartered airliner on weekends for their only opportunity for regular daytime activity with family and friends.

The Navy, too, has long recognized the value of Nevada's attributes of sweeping wilderness and boundless sky. Fearing coastal raids in the wake of the Japanese attack on Pearl Harbor, new airfields were quickly erected sufficiently inland, in Nevada's desert region, to give a cushion of protection. The Navy developed a continuing presence at one of these airfields, near the small town of Fallon, which is about fifty miles east of Reno. Today, like its Air Force counterpart to the south, Naval Air Station Fallon controls enormous blocks of airspace over Nevada's wide-ranging desert territory. For its training requirements and to ensure safety, the air station's authority extends over nearly a quarter million acres.

When it was announced that the Marine Corps air station at El Toro in southern California was closing with many of its assets being transferred to the Miramar Naval Air Station relatively nearby, the Navy decided it needed a new home for its illustrious Fighter Weapons School, popularly known as Top Gun. Fallon, already home to a cutting-edge naval air operation and surrounded by wide open spaces in the neighboring state, made an emi-

nently reasonable choice. Because the Navy's Strike Warfare School was already at Fallon, the fighter types co-locating with their air-to-ground cohorts resulted in the formation of what is now referred to as the Naval Strike and Air Warfare Center. Thanks in large part to shrinking defense budgets and unimpeded real-estate development with its attendant encroachment on the West Coast, this fusion of Fightertown with Strike U occurred in 1996.

The integrated air warfare training at Fallon accommodates up to five carrier-based air wings every year with short courses on the ground and in the air geared towards preparing flight crews and support personnel for combat from the sea. About 40,000 Navy men and women pass through Fallon's training programs in an average year, attesting to the considerable import of Nevada's consistently favorable flying conditions. Although little known outside the tightly knit naval air community, Fallon plays a major role in ensuring the readiness of aviators and flight officers for their demanding missions. When Hornets and Tomcats are seen on cable news channels catapulting from or trapping on carrier decks in pitching seas as part of no-fly-zone patrols or embassy extraction missions, chances are that the flight crews learned valuable lessons in the usually cloudless ranges controlled by Naval Air Station Fallon.

The air station's proximity to Reno virtually guarantees that combat jets home-based at Fallon will join in the air-show portion of the air races. The jets from Fallon tend to stand out, for the ones sent to the air races have generally been decorated in a desert camouflage scheme incorporating different shadings of brown, from light to dark. This is a departure from the standard low-visibility gray. When these strike-fighters roar into the sky on take-off, their distinctive colors quickly blend into the buckskin foothills, demonstrating the effectiveness of their specially devised surface coatings.

Where Cleveland and Ohio are representative of the Midwest as an incubator of aviation, Reno and Nevada are indicative of the West as executor. It was perhaps predictable that the core of aviation would shift from areas of crowding populace and changeable weather patterns to a region of uninterrupted space and methodically clear skies. When the features that once made California sparkle as the logical center of the aerospace industry began to dim, a shift back in the opposite direction took place. The move backwards was but one step that positioned the players in the remaining wide open spaces of the country – the vast and lonely, arid acreage depicted in earthen tones on the western quadrant of the national map.

Not surprisingly, when a new set of air races was promoted in the mid-1990s, the location chosen was the southwestern desert state of Arizona. The Phoenix 500 air races held at Williams Gateway Airport, which had been an Air Force training base on the periphery of the metropolitan area, attempted to increase the exposure of air racing and to give the coterie of racing pilots an additional opportunity for fame and fortune. But developing the bedrock for additional, free-standing races proved too difficult.

Securing ongoing corporate sponsorship and generating a sufficiently sized purse to attract the racers were goals of those organizing the Phoenix air races. It appeared that all the ingredients existed to make the envisioned new air races a success. Phoenix is a much larger community than Reno, so it was reasonable to assume that the attendance would be proportionately larger, which, in turn, led to expectations of more sponsorship by companies seeking to publicize their products and services in front of live audiences. Also, logic would suggest that by running their high-powered aircraft in more than a single competition during the year, the owners and operators of the unlimited racers would achieve an economy of scale. Plans called for making the Phoenix 500 a multi-faceted entertainment attraction with a musical component and other features normally associated with non-flying sports and entertainment events.

Problems included the failure to consistently draw one of the North American military jet teams. Without such a headline act, to borrow from the industry's jargon, attendance drops off noticeably. The loss of a Corsair early on caused a reworking of the unlimited course to enhance safety. This change restricted the turning radius of competing racers and thereby limited their speeds, effectively precluding any chance of matching, let alone exceeding, already established records. Moreover, the owners and operators, after initially warming to the possibility of another venue, lost interest. The available purse apparently did not rise to a level that would be enticing.

Reno has always been a grassroots phenomenon, steeped in the aviation of the individual much like the pre-war air races at Cleveland. By contrast, the Phoenix 500 burst onto the scene as a stratagem devised by professional promoters who, at least on the surface, left nothing to chance in an effort to duplicate the success of the Reno air races. But as is often the case in such undertakings, the intangibles become dominant. Given the disparity in origins of the two air racing events, one might conclude that the premature demise of the Phoenix 500 resulted, at least in part, from a paucity of soul. At Reno, the driving force was and continues to be a passion for flight at the edge of the proverbial envelope, the inimitable sights and sounds of airplanes rumbling around pylons, the fusing of man and machine in an airborne rush.

Obviously not suffering from superstition, Robert Jones of Kerman, California steeply banks his Pitts Special, *One Arm Bandit.* In the 2000 Gold Biplane Class, Jones came in fifth with an average speed of 183.245 mph. The biplane racers are always the second class to race each day so as to take advantage of the usually calmer air of the September mornings. (*2000*)

Imperceptibly, over time, the partisans who come each year to root for their favorites have developed into an army of supporters, a foundation girding the event. While the head count at the Reno air races on a given day usually does not exceed 50,000, that number contains a diehard element. And out at the pylons and along the perimeter fence, a corps of volunteers has emerged, quiet and proud, just glad to be there on race days, shuttling the media, guarding the course, judging the competitors. There is an irreplaceable bawdy authenticity underlying the Reno air races, personified, for example, in the everyday ambience of the pit area, and at the after-races dinner in the low-ceilinged hangar shared by the formula and biplane racers.

The air-racing scene is constantly charged with talk about the need for more over-arching sponsorship such as that which buttresses stock car racing, corporate behemoths peddling their brands of beer or tobacco with recognizable logos stretched across banners and spread over barrier walls. Then, too, there is the incessant pining for comprehensive television coverage by a major network, with the presumed exposure that would entail for the otherwise insular sport of air racing.

Somehow, the Reno air races have been able to flourish in the absence of the promotional pillars many consider essential for success in the public arena today. Ironically, this locale, which came to national prominence through the hoopla and exhibitionism of its burgeoning casinos, hosts air racing, a thrilling adventure of the most unpretentious and earthy kind. No one wears makeup on the flight line; under the intense heat it would just dissolve in rivulets of sweat anyway. Moms and dads bring their children, and together they scour the multitude of vendors, selecting the right memento – a hat, T-shirt, or poster – by which to remember the exuberant day. Air-racing luminaries, clad in fire-retardant flight suits, are seen meandering among the spectators near the pits, slurping at fast-melting ice-cream bars.

One of the greatest pilots of all time, popular with the crowds and a regular at the air races, is easily recognizable by his matchless saunter and signature sombrero. Tall and lanky, the legendary Robert R. A. 'Bob' Hoover carries himself with an aura of self-confidence. He can honestly claim to have flown as wingman to Chuck Yeager, including the famous mission in 1947 when Yeager became the first man to break through the foreboding sound barrier. Indeed, Hoover's life, after harrowing experiences as a captured fighter pilot during World War II, has been devoted to the remarkable worlds of flight testing and air shows.

At Wright-Patterson Air Force Base and then at Edwards Air Force Base, Hoover reveled in wringing out whatever aircraft happened to occupy the ramp, tearing up the skies in mock dogfights with his flying partner Yeager. They were an incredible team, neither one ever able to outdo the other in simulated air combat. The lure of industry was irresistible, though, and in 1948 Hoover left the military and went to work for several businesses, his tenure at North American Aviation the most notable. He flew various models of the F-86 Sabre, and as a company technical representative he even participated in combat missions during the Korean War, earning the lasting admiration of those Air Force fighter pilots with whom he flew.

Performing at air shows was a natural extension of his flying. For the next four decades, Hoover's precision aerial displays graced the skies at air shows all over the U.S. Jimmy Doolittle, looking back over a lifetime of flying, paid the ultimate compliment when he remarked that Bob Hoover was the greatest stick-and-rudder man he had ever known. Hoover has been a regular at the Reno air races from the beginning. He not only performed in the flying displays, but piloted the pace plane in the unlimited heats. Indeed, he is credited with originating the distinctive call that signaled the start of the unlimited contests. From the privi-

leged perspective of the cockpit of his pace plane, where he could behold the powerful racers lined up and raring to go, he would call out 'Gentlemen, you have a race!' Then, with a yank on the control stick, he would pull up. The racers plunged forward in a free-for-all, unleashing the full might of their engines and jockeying for position out of the chute.

For the next several minutes, the course belonged to the racers, and if any experienced a blown valve or a ruptured oil line, the steady voice of a pioneer test pilot intoned from the airspace high above to guide the stricken bird back to its nest. This is what Hoover did so well. He had participated in the early days of post-war flight testing, when exotic shapes in the famed X-series of research planes were getting off the ground – literally. Maydays were common then, and he brought a cool reserve to the hot seat, establishing, along with his test pilot brethren, the rubric for later generations of test pilots.

With over 300 different aircraft recorded in his logbook, he has piloted more types than almost anyone else. He is believed to have accumulated more hours performing in front of more fans than any other air-show pilot. It is also generally acknowledged that Bob Hoover has escaped from more life-threatening incidents in the air than any other flyer. When the Federal Aviation Administration revoked his medical certificate on highly questionable grounds in the 1990s, he did not respond passively. He launched a spirited campaign that was widely supported by fellow pilots and aviation organizations. Not only did he obtain the reinstatement of his medical certificate, but new federal legislation was adopted to temper the FAA's emergency revocation powers.

Ironically, during the time that he was officially grounded in the U.S., he was flying in many other countries with a license granted by Australia. His air-show routine was as popular with foreign audiences as with the droves of Americans who had grown up watching him delicately loop and roll with unwavering exactitude. He still came to Reno in those years when governmental decree precluded his flying above home soil, and the crowds swarmed all over him, passing on words of encouragement and gesturing with thumbs up. Rather than sit out the races, he hitched a ride as a passenger in the pace plane so that he could deliver his famous call to start the unlimited racers. His familiar voice lent consistency to the races. It was as if nothing had changed.

When, finally, his appeals wore down the bureaucracy, he returned to the sky over Reno, cavorting, as if it were yesterday, in his green-and-white Shrike Commander. The revered fixture who had been missing for a few years from the air show at Reno was back, executing his trademark maneuvers with the same skill, grace, and sureness as always. The plane arced high, spewing twin columns of white smoke, and then by design one of the white smoke trails dissipated, a signal that one of the two engines was cut off. A short while later in the routine, the second engine was shut down; both the remaining plume of white smoke and the engine sound vanished. Only the swish of the aircraft riding its inherent energy, like a glider gushing against the wind, could be heard across the unusually quiet show line.

In masterful strokes of airmanship, the Great One, as Hoover's air-show announcer, live microphone in hand, immodestly referred to him, dead-sticked the plane to a greaser of a landing, right on the numbers. Moreover, with the residual energy, he taxied to a pre-designated spot about midway along the show line, compensating for wind, pavement grade, and the like, and then applied the brakes, coming to rest exactly where planned. The uninitiated who were attending a Bob Hoover performance for the first time might be suckered into betting against the old test pilot reaching the parking place without power, but I never saw any of those unlucky patsies repeat their mistake.

The air-show season for the year 2000 brought another challenge for Bob Hoover. Insurance coverage for his flying was not readily available, so he found himself grounded again, at least for the time being. However, true to form, he came to Reno and, wearing his easily identifiable yellow flight suit with green trim patterned after the color scheme of his old P-51 Mustang, allocated more time to greeting well-wishers, selling toy models of his airplanes and signing copies of his popular autobiography. Those who know Bob Hoover, indeed the many aviation enthusiasts who have been stirred by the excellence of his flying, suspect that as long as the Great One is still breathing he will find a way to get airborne again. The Reno air races are just not the same without him dancing in the sky.

Peeling Pylons: Flying Fast, Staying Tight

The desert wakes slowly. A hardly perceptible unwrapping of the night-time darkness presages the dawn, pervaded by an exhilarating stillness as the first hint of light peeks ever so gently over the horizon. That blush of luminosity carries hope, an unembellished freshness, a sense of renewal across the solitude. Standing at the pylons under the limitless sky at daybreak, an amber glow radiating off the surrounding mountains and the flowering sage emitting its aromatic fragrance, a sense of majestic eternity inspires one to relish life and its infinite possibilities. The medium, pristine and calm, beckons, and soon the blue dome fills with frantic racers, their pilots reaching beyond the norms into the realm of the extraordinary.

Of the five operative racing classes in the year 2000, only the Formula and Biplane Classes share the same course, which is the shortest at only 3.1195 miles. The AT-6 course is proportionately larger at 4.9616 miles. The relatively new class of sport planes has a 6.3089-mile course. By far the longest course, 8.2688 miles, belongs to the Unlimited Class. All the courses have an oval shape except the course for the Sport Class, which comes close to being a perfect circle.

For the first three official air-racing days, always Thursday through Saturday, each class except Formula One has fewer laps to

The newest racing class at Reno is for so-called sport planes, which may use engines of up to 650 cubic inches displacement. These are known as the carbon racers since they make significant use of carbon composites in their construction. This Sport Class racer is a Glasair IIs TD owned and piloted by P. Earl Hibler of Hayward, California. It is unusual for the class in that most of the racers are retractable tricycle-gear planes like the Lancair IV and the Questair Venture. Nicknamed *Baby Doll*, this racer finished third in the 2000 Silver race with an average speed of 256.885 mph. (*2000*)

complete in the heats than on the final race day, always a Sunday. The biplanes and AT-6s have five-lap races until Sunday, when these classes are assigned one more lap. The Sport Class goes from six laps to seven laps while the Unlimited Class jumps from six laps to eight laps. Formula racers have eight laps to complete on all four official race days.

Earlier in the week, Monday through Wednesday, qualifications are held with each racer given the opportunity to run two timing laps. The faster of the two laps is used for qualification purposes. Only so many planes may enter the official races in each class: twenty-four in the Unlimited, Formula, and Biplane; eighteen in the AT-6; and sixteen in the Sport. Aircraft registering the fastest speeds in the timing laps become the qualifiers. Those eliminated during qualifications may in some cases be used as alternates should the need arise.

Starting positions hinge initially on qualifying speeds, with the fastest planes getting the 'pole' position. As the races unfold, starting positions are determined by speeds obtained in the various races of the immediately preceding day. A race progression system applies during the four days of official races so that planes demonstrating similar speeds are lumped together in heats. Basically, the better-performing aircraft keep moving up the matrix until only the fastest are left for the bronze, silver, and gold races on the last day.

The Biplane and Formula Class races are started on the ground. These petite aircraft, the bantamweights of air racing, are aligned on the runway almost like horses at Pimlico or Belmont, and launch into their take-off rolls when a race official standing to the side dramatically lowers a green flag. All of a sudden, when the flag drops, the engines rev up palpably, like a collection of buzz-saws, and the racers dart off into the air, quickly scattering by the time they make their way to the first pylon.

All other classes use an air start. The aircraft competing in a given heat take off individually and then form up on the pace plane, which usually maintains high visibility by emitting puffs of white smoke. The pace plane keeps the racers in a line-abreast formation all the way to the entry point to the racecourse, ensuring that all participants stay aligned until the race is started with that time-honored staccato call: 'Gentlemen, you have a race!' Because women are competing increasingly in these classes, the starting call is modified when necessary. Of course, any racer pulling ahead of the formation before the call is severely penalized.

In a wise move, beginning in 1998, race officials decided to hold training sessions once a year at Reno/Stead Airport for first-time pilots to the sport of air racing and for veterans wanting a refresher in the fundamentals. The seminar-like experience is crammed into a busy extended weekend that takes place a few months prior to the races, a time that allows for a more conducive environment for acquainting the would-be competitors with the fundamentals of flying in the races. The rules of the racecourse are imparted along with flying techniques and safety procedures. Instructors are not ivory-tower academicians, but experienced racing pilots, their names recognizable and respected among those taking the lessons.

Race competitors must participate in this training if they have had a lay-off from air racing for three or more years. Also, a pilot's change from one racing class to another necessitates enrollment. The ground instruction is augmented by flight on the actual racecourse. This is particularly helpful for the newcomers as it gives them a way to familiarize themselves with the lay-out of the course without the tension of an actual race. At the end of the weekend, the instructors review each candidate. Obtaining an affirmative nod from the faculty is a requirement for competing at Reno in September.

At the ground school, pilots learn that their planes are not permitted to dip below the pylons, which stand about forty feet above the desert floor. Specifically, the pylon judges, positioned at the base of every pylon on race days, scrutinizing the racers as they swing around, will penalize a contestant if his or her eye level sinks below the top of any pylon. Conversely, contestants are prohibited from exceeding an altitude of 1,500 feet above ground level. However, should an emergency develop during a race, the contestant may exceed the upper-altitude restriction. If the contestant declares a mayday, he or she is then precluded from re-entering the race that is underway. Typically, when maydays are declared (and there have been races in which half the contenders do so) the affected aircraft climb hurriedly and substantially on the premise that excess altitude is 'money in the bank'. With the extra space between them and the ground, the pilots in stricken planes have more time to assess the problem and set up for a landing, including a dead-stick landing in the event of an engine failure. The pace plane, orbiting overhead, can assist the disabled aircraft by performing a visual check or by guiding it to a landing over the air-racing frequency.

Reno/Stead Airport has two active runways, each more than sufficient in length at 7,600 feet and 8,080 feet respectively. Both measure a comfortable 150 feet in width. There is a maze of asphalt surfaces consisting of crisscrossing taxiways and even an old closed runway. This is important because the pilots of racing planes experiencing an emergency look for the closest hard surface on which to roll out. When seconds matter, an abandoned runway rippled with cracks and crevices may be just fine for getting back onto the ground in one piece. Sometimes, extenuating circumstances have necessitated an immediate pancaking onto the desert floor, metal incongruously rubbing against the sagebrush. Usually, though, pilots declaring a mayday manage to maneuver onto one of the runways, recovering without incident. Commonly, up to three in-flight emergencies occur during a race day.

A real concern is that a mid-air collision may occur, given that the racers have been known to bunch up in clusters during an air start and when rounding pylons. Indeed, while rare, this scenario has happened, with gruesome consequences, so reckless jockeying is severely frowned upon. No one may jump ahead of the pack before the start of the race is called. Cutting pylons is strictly forbidden, a pylon cut being defined as flying inside a pylon or having any part of the racing aircraft banking over a pylon. The judges impose a harsh penalty of two seconds per lap for each instance of pylon cutting. However, a rule-abiding contestant who is crowded into cutting a pylon by another race participant flying too aggressively will not be penalized.

Aerobatic prowess is among the essential skills for air racing in that the turbulent air of the late afternoon, roiled by racers churning up the currents around the course, can disrupt the stability of a contestant's plane, requiring quick and extreme maneuvering to restore normal attitude. Also, having ability in formation flying is mandatory. Racing pilots have to know how to turn tight in close proximity to other planes yet keep those competitors in sight. These attributes are encouraged and honed during the training weekend. The goal of the instruction is not to pass on tips for winning, but to instill safe flying practices.

You've Got Class: A Multitude of Propeller Types

Biplane Class

For lovers of propeller-driven aircraft, there is something for everyone in the air racing at Reno. The tiny sport biplanes tend to be evenly matched, and although they do not make the noise or generate the crowds of the aircraft in the heavier air-racing classes, they make for some exciting finishes. Most of the aircraft in the Biplane Class are variations of the Pitts Special, an excellent aerobatic platform in wide use throughout the world. There are sprinklings of other biplane types in the class, including the Mong Sport and the Smith Mini Plane. Once in a while, a unique design pops up on the circuit, like the Rose Peregrine.

Winning speeds for the biplane racers progressed from the early years of the mid-1960s to a point by the mid-1970s where they were nibbling at the 200 mph mark. When that plateau was finally surpassed in 1976, expectations were elevated for subsequent races. By 1983, a record for the Biplane Class was set with a winning speed of 217.60 mph. Interestingly, in the years that have followed, the closest anyone has come to matching that all-time highest speed was in 1996 with a speed that fell short by nearly 5 mph.

Formula One Class

The Formula One Class is comprised mainly of Cassutt racers, tiny mid-wing aircraft that look like they could hardly accommodate a full-grown adult in the cockpit. The tail surfaces are so minuscule, they could be mistaken for parts from a radio-controlled model plane. When the formula racers whiz around the racecourse, they sound like lawn mowers revved up to the highest possible pitch. It could be said that the pilots of these planes are strapping on a set of wings and an engine.

Incredibly, for nine straight years, from 1991 to 1999, the Formula One Class was dominated by a single pilot, Jon Sharp, and his aircraft, the constantly tweaked *Nemesis*. Combined with two earlier Formula One victories in another aircraft, Sharp chalked up a total of eleven wins. An engineer at the Lockheed Martin Skunk Works, Sharp applied his cutting-edge expertise to the design of his custom racer. A one-of-a-kind design, *Nemesis* set the speed record in the class in 1995, zipping along at 249.904 mph. Constructed entirely of carbon fiber, it is light yet sturdy.

With such a long unbroken winning streak, and with his winning speeds having topped out at mid-decade, Sharp decided to move on to another racing class. Starting in 2001, he expects to

In 1998, Reno air-racing officials decided to initiate a whole new class just for T-28 trainers predicated in part on interest developed a few years earlier at the Phoenix 500. The theory was that these old radial-engine former Air Force and Navy aircraft, which are still relatively plentiful, would provide some evenly matched races, as happens in the AT-6 Class. Unfortunately, the T-28 Class lasted only a single year at Reno. Racing enthusiasts who enjoy the rattling of these flying washing machines are hoping for an eventual return of the class. (*1998*)

enter a brand-new racer of his design in the Sport Class. Called *Nemesis NXT*, this two-seat racer will feature the same type of composite materials as found in the original *Nemesis*, incorporate retractable landing gear, and be powered by a turbo-charged Continental 550 horsepower engine. Sharp has announced that the new plane will be available for purchase as a kit.

As for the unbeaten *Nemesis*, Sharp flew it for the last time at the Experimental Aircraft Association's annual AirVenture in Oshkosh, Wisconsin in 2000. Upon landing, he turned it over to representatives of the Smithsonian Institution's National Air and Space Museum. In the meantime, the famous aircraft will reside on loan in the EAA's AirVenture Museum. When the National Air and Space Museum opens its new display center at Dulles International Airport in Virginia in 2003, the year of powered flight's centennial, *Nemesis* will move there for permanent exhibition.

Sport Class

The Sport Class is the newest racing category, having started up in 1998. It is populated by Lancairs, Questairs, and Glasairs. Like the Formula One Class, the Sport Class offers a lot of innovation in materials and structures. However, in contrast to the formula racers, the sport plane types have real utility in the world of every-day flying. They have a place for a second seat for a passenger and meaningful range for cross-country trips. Indeed, with the flowering in the 1990s of practical and fast new designs for the general aviation community, it only made sense for the Reno air racing authorities to include these kinds of planes in a class of their own.

Dramatically streamlined and using composite materials, the sport planes represent a new design philosophy for the kinds of aircraft flown by private pilots. The traditional piston-powered airplanes produced by the established manufacturers have by and large remained unchanged over decades. The shapes and performance specifications of such aircraft have stagnated. The sport planes are instead the products of upstart companies challenging the status quo and seeking to push the level of expectations. Many of the parts and even the powerplants are off the shelf, but they are put together in unconventional ways that boost performance.

In the first three years of Sport Class racing, David Morss has won in a Lancair IV, setting progressively faster speeds each time. In 2000, his winning speed was a sizzling 328.045 mph.

AT-6 Class

Although recent winning speeds are about 100 mph less than in the Sport Class, crowds continue to favor AT-6 Class racers, perhaps proving that speed is only one element in the popularity of racing classes. Old-fashioned, plump, metallic, and loud, the AT-6/SNJ Texans are remnants of an earlier era. When America needed an advanced trainer to graduate hordes of cadets for a raging war, it turned to North American Aviation's husky design. A classic configuration of low-wing, greenhouse canopy, radial engine, and tailwheel, this magnificent airplane was produced in the thousands to meet the enormous training demand. Demonstrating the independence of the U.S. military's branches of service, the Army's designation was AT-6 and the Navy's designation was SNJ.

The primary and basic trainers like the PT-17 Kaydet, usually called the Stearman, and the BT-13 Valiant, commonly referred to as the Vibrator, taught the fundamentals of airmanship. If a student made it through those stages of flight training, his final test came when he mounted the AT-6/SNJ, a plane calculated to weed out those lacking in flying aptitude. The student now had to master faster speeds, instruments, and complex systems. The thought was that if someone could fly this airplane, he could fly virtually anything in the military's inventory. The U.S. military's official nickname for the aircraft was Texan, and in the British Commonwealth it was known as the Harvard. Fittingly, many called it simply the 'Pilot Maker'.

The AT-6 Class is the ultimate in evenly matched racers. These planes, more than those of any other class, clump up in bunches rounding the pylons as they are equal in almost every respect. Their nine-cylinder Pratt & Whitney engines pound away, turning the short-bladed propellers at a furious tempo, which generates the thumping sound distinctive to the Texan/Harvard.

Winning speeds for the AT-6 racers have not varied more than 21 mph through the 1980s and 1990s. Never a truly fast plane, the AT-6, when handled expertly on the closed course at Reno, can get up to a maximum of a number just to the plus side of 200 mph. There really is not much room for enhancing the upper limits since race officials do not permit any significant race-related modifications on the AT-6 racers. The peak was achieved in 1992 when Eddie Van Fossen rode his *Miss TNT* to a dazzling victory at 234.766 mph. In 2000, Nick Macy won with a respectable 228.299 mph in *Six-Cat*.

Unlimited Class

The ultimate air-racing planes, the unlimiteds, are fighters of World War II vintage. At the outset of the new millennium, the unlimited racing line-up largely comprises Mustangs and Sea Furies. In recent years, there have also been a few other types such as Bearcats and Russian Yaks. In the history of the Reno air races, a wide array of fighter planes, from Warhawks to Thunderbolts, has entered the Unlimited Class. Additionally, attempts were made to field scratch-built racers in the class, but these promising one-of-a-kind aircraft did not survive long enough to fulfill their potential.

Almost every year, there is talk of newly modified fighters or futuristic designs underway at places like Chino or Mojave in southern California. The intensity of the labor and the magnitude of the cost limit the number of projects that reach fruition. Nevertheless, dreams of swept aluminum wings sparkling under the Reno sun and the notion of pushing the speed envelope ever closer to the edge keep the entrepreneurial spirit alive in ramshackle hangars and engine shops.

In the months leading up to the races, one can roam the fun airports away from the big cities that are vital to the warbird and sport aviation movement. Here, you can poke your head through an open door and gaze at dazzling shapes and gaudy color combinations, the bold creations being prepped for Reno. Although not all will make it to the flight line, it is no less thrilling to see such handiwork. Clipped wings, razorback canopies, glossy finish coats, and shiny spinners evolve from an active imagination and an ardor for aviation. Even when parked with cowling panels removed, these racers exude power and acceleration, as if to say they belong not on the pavement but in the sky, aloft in the more natural surroundings of the ocean of air.

And some of the pilots are as colorful as their planes. A perennial favorite at the Reno air races was Texas cropduster and World War II Army Air Force veteran Marvin 'Lefty' Gardner. After the war, in which Gardner flew both B-24 and B-17 bombers, he stayed in flying by operating an aerial applicator business. The planes used were war-surplus items that could be purchased for a fraction of today's values. When the day's work was done, the fields sprayed in the methodical way of cropdusting pilots, Gardner would hop into one of his bargain-priced fighters and gyrate through the sky for entertainment. Air-show flying and air racing were natural extensions of Gardner's aviation background. By its nature, cropdusting involves flying at the extremes of an airplane's capabilities, performing tight turns at high power settings close to the ground – perfect preparation for the Reno kind of flying.

Gardner's preferred show plane was his extremely rare P-38L Lightning, called *White Lightnin'* because of its atypical paint scheme of white with blue and red trim. The aircraft, which emerged in the late 1930s from the talented design team at Lockheed, featured a twin-boom configuration with counter-rotating propellers to negate torque effect (the tendency of a whirling propeller to pull the nose of an airplane in a given direction, usually to the left). This meant that the fighter was an unusually stable gun platform. With all its firepower, comprised of four .50-caliber machine guns and one 20 mm cannon, concentrated in the nose, the plane was a formidable weapon. It was the aircraft type flown by America's highest-scoring ace, Richard Bong.

For years, *White Lightnin'* graced the skies at Reno and other air shows across the western states. Gardner piloted the plane in flying displays as if it were an inseparable part of himself. Smooth in every facet of a maneuver, Gardner practically made air-show flying synonymous with ballet. He would execute one part of a Cuban Eight to one side of the show line and then come back and complete it in the opposite direction with such precision that if you had held up a huge mirror to detect any deviation it would have been negligible.

As part of his finale, he would input cross controls and the magnificent fighter, that fork-tailed devil, as the Japanese referred to it, turned knife-edge, the overhead planform exposed to the crowd along the show line. Gardner would hold the controls just so, and the Lightning kind of slid sideways for the length of the show line, the amazing sight of Reno's pure blue framed in a near perfect square by the fighter's structure standing on its wingtip. One can imagine Tony LeVier, the outstanding Lockheed test pilot and early racing pilot, performing similar maneuvers with the same gifted touch during World War II for the benefit of Army fighter pilots who had doubts initially about the handling characteristics of this unconventional design. For sky and machine, it was as though nothing had changed over all the years since the war. The same beautiful airplane at the command of an able pilot traced elegant lines in the open space above as spectators gaped in awe.

The perennial underdog yet always the popular favorite, Marvin 'Lefty' Gardner entertained Reno air-racing fans with spirited pylon runs during the unlimited heats and graceful displays during the air-show portions of the event. His Lockheed P-38L Lightning, *White Lightnin'*, was a regular at Reno. By the late 1990s, Gardner, a World War II bomber pilot who had yearned to fly fighters, retired from the racing and show circuit. (*Phoenix 1995*)

At Reno, the crowds often enjoyed a double treat since in addition to performing in the air show, Gardner would enter *White Lightnin'* in the unlimited races. The plane was conceived as a high-altitude interceptor so it was not the fastest racer around the Reno pylons, but Gardner developed a reputation as a gritty competitor; he hugged the pylons closer than any of the unlimited pilots. Sometimes he would get so close, it looked like his port wingtip would scrape the paint off the pylons. Standing at the base of a pylon, you could actually see the whites of Gardner's eyes. That is close!

A little like a rock star or a symphony conductor, Gardner, the unaffected cropduster from the prairie lands of Texas who was always happy to put his arm around you and amuse you with stories of life on the go as a cropduster, had a loyal following. The crowds and even the media cheered him on. Back in 1976, flying a Mustang, he won the Gold Championship. The flying always more important than the winning, he kept performing and racing through most of the 1990s, even a few years after he said he had retired. Finally, the inescapable fact of age set in for this folksy gentleman of the World War II generation who always spoke plainly in a pronounced southern drawl, and he really did retire, leaving the Reno air races devoid of one of its immortal airmen.

The contest for the Unlimited Gold is in part a competition between the big air-cooled monsters like the Hawker Sea Furies and the sleek liquid-cooled racers like the North American Mustangs. Indeed, in 2000, the first six finishers in the Gold Championship race were alternately Mustangs and Sea Furies. The winner by a wide margin was longtime entrant and previous victor *Dago Red*, a highly modified P-51D which, in 2000, recorded the sixth fastest winning course speed in history at 462.007 mph. Experienced racing pilot and previous Gold Champion Skip Holm was at the controls.

Dynasties: Faster and Faster

The Unlimited Class at the Reno air races has been characterized in the early years, and again in recent years, by dynasties of particularly fast planes. From the second year of the Reno air races in 1965 through the end of the decade, all the Gold Championship races were won by Darryl Greenamyer, one of the grand old men of air racing who has set speed records for both piston and jet aircraft. Greenamyer's run in the 1960s represents the longest uninterrupted winning streak in unlimited racing history. Moreover, Greenamyer came back in 1971 and 1977 to capture the gold, bringing his overall victory count to seven.

Since 1987, the class has been dominated by three racers: Bill 'Tiger' Destefani's Mustang *Strega*, Lyle Shelton's Bearcat *Rare Bear*, and the Mustang *Dago Red* flown by Bruce Lockwood and Skip Holm. In the fourteen Unlimited Gold races between 1987 and 2000, these three planes achieved winning speeds that ranged anywhere from about 20 mph to 40 mph above the highest speeds recorded at Reno in prior years.

The all-time racing record for the closed course at Reno was set in 1991 by Lyle Shelton in his *Rare Bear* with a speed of 481.618 mph. This eye-popping accomplishment has not yet come under serious challenge; as the next closest speed, 472.332 mph, was reached by Bruce Lockwood flying *Dago Red* in 1999. Yet some believe that the success of *Rare Bear* in expanding the speed envelope so meaningfully suggests that it might be possible for someone eventually to break through the 500 mph mark on the closed course. So far, such speeds for piston aircraft have only been obtainable on straightaways. On 21 August 1989, over a three-kilometer straight course in New Mexico, *Rare Bear* established the record for piston aircraft with a speed dash of 528.329 mph.

These extraordinary planes zooming around the pylons at Reno are hardly the stock fighters that rolled off production lines during or shortly after World War II. For example, in the case of *Rare Bear*, a Grumman Bearcat built as a Navy/Marine carrier-qualified fighter, the standard Pratt & Whitney powerplant was replaced with a Wright engine. That engine's output was boosted by Lyle Shelton's team of mechanics from the normal 2,400 horsepower to more than 4,000 horsepower.

In fact, it is precisely because the engines in the hottest racers are tweaked and operated at such extremes for the few minutes of a competition heat that they are temperamental and prone to malfunction. Indeed, mechanical problems, entailing wallet-busting expenses and labor-intensive repairs, plagued *Rare Bear* and *Strega* in the closing years of the last century and the first year of the new millennium, which opened the way for *Dago Red* to assume the championship title. It is worth noting that the capriciousness of these substantially altered engines is in stark contrast to the highly reliable assembly-line versions of Pratts, Merlins, Allisons, etc. produced en masse for World War II era fighters.

For more than the last decade, then, the universe of genuine contenders for the Unlimited Gold has been confined to a handful of well-known regulars, the uncertainty as to the outcome of the modern races considerably reduced, but still no one knows a priori which of the smattering of superlative racers will triumph. If nothing else, mechanical difficulties, arising in the final seconds of the last lap of the Gold race, may intervene to quash a racer's chances, sending statistical probabilities aimed at predicting a winner into a tailspin.

The dynasty of *Strega* has seesawed in stages, starting with a win in 1987, then resuming with back-to-back wins in 1992 and 1993, and coming back for a three-year run from 1995 through 1997. *Rare Bear* was the winner in all the off-years from 1988 up to and including 1994. When both of these planes started to encounter new rounds of expensive maintenance issues, *Dago Red*, a Gold Champion in 1982, re-emerged as a freshly modified contender in 1998.

There is a finite supply of piston fighters, and it seems that each year the quantity dwindles because of accidents necessitating the write-off of a few. The trend at this time is for the venerable racers of the past to be remade with new engines, cooling systems, streamlining, etc. with an eye towards their becoming serious challengers. While there have been a couple of novel designs entered into the Unlimited Class, it is surprising that no one has been able to create a contender from scratch that outperforms the old fighters. Until that day comes, it will remain a stunning verity that the aeronautical design community of World War II, more than half a century ago, devised the quintessential airframes for piston-powered fighters.

Since the first Unlimited Gold race at Reno in 1964, when Mira Slovak won with a speed of 376.84 mph, winning speeds have been on a mainly upward progression, topping out at slightly more than 100 mph above that first year's winning speed. One of the notable milestones was reached in 1969 when Darryl Greenamyer penetrated the 400-mph mark for the first time at the races, attaining a speed of 412.63 mph in his Bearcat *Conquest 1*. With only three exceptions, all winning speeds in the Unlimited Class since then have exceeded 400 mph. After winning the Unlimited Gold in 2000, Skip Holm attempted to break through the thus far impregnable 500-mph barrier on the Reno course, but technical problems impeded him.

The Gold race experience is spine-tingling. At the eastern-most pylon in the late afternoon, a row of tiny specks in line-abreast formation first becomes visible from around the distant mountain peak when the rays of the waning sun glint off the approaching machines. As if portending the onslaught of the thundering herd, gusts of wind kick up, rattling the tin atop the forty-foot-high pylon. Swirls of sand, called dust devils, lifted from the surface of the heated desert by the contorted wind, dance over the sagebrush in apparent aimlessness, bombarding bystanders with countless infinitesimal particles, causing hats to be whisked away and eyes to tear. It is an apt reminder just before the start of the race is called as to the forces influencing the outcome.

Can it be that those far-off dots are massive hulks of formed metal roaring at breakneck speeds? In what seems an interminable amount of time, the pinpoints out there begin to take shape. They are getting closer. At the designated spot in the air, we hear a crackling transmission over the bevy of handheld transceivers tuned to race frequency. It is the excited refrain from the pace plane, the call everyone on the ramp, at the pylons, and in the air

has been waiting for: 'Gentlemen, you have a race!' With barely a pause, the controller on board the pace plane repeats once more the call 'You have a race!', as if to ensure that a command to commence firing has been heard and understood by the frontline troops.

On cue, the pace plane pulls up dramatically, spewing a trail of white smoke. There is no doubt now; the race has begun, and the contestants stream headlong towards the first pylon, no longer neatly aligned but scattering for position. The racing planes in all their majestic glory growl past in an instant, the unique paint schemes and shimmering, polished aluminum surfaces receding as fast as they came into view, churning up the air currents, intensifying the already squally wind gusts.

Inside the cockpits, pilots wrestle with the choppy air caused by

In 1999, the Reno Air Racing Association, which oversees the air races, linked up with the National Aviation Hall of Fame, the Smithsonian Institution's National Air and Space Museum, and Rolls-Royce North America to begin recognizing annually the best restoration of an antique aircraft with the awarding of the Rolls-Royce Aviation Heritage Trophy. This historically significant F2G-1D Super Corsair, emblazoned in its authentic 1949 Cleveland air-racing colors, was painstakingly refurbished and detailed by Bob Odegaard of Kindred, North Dakota. While airworthy and a beauty to behold in the sky, it is now a show plane, no longer a racer. Indeed, eligibility requirements mandate that any aircraft under consideration for the trophy shall not participate in the Reno air races. (1999)

the afternoon thermals billowing from the sun-baked desert floor. The pilots must not allow these distractions to lure their attention; they must concentrate on the next pylon, their waypoint in this intense promenade – always the next pylon. Simultaneously, they have to monitor their propulsive systems, scanning the oil pressure, oil temperature, and manifold pressure read-outs as well as the tachometer, adjusting the throttle setting and the propeller's pitch depending on conditions that change in split seconds. With high power settings, the intrepid airmen have their steeds trimmed nose-low to counteract the tendency of an airplane to point upward and climb with the throttle shoved forward. At near maximum speed, the racers respond quickly to even delicate control inputs. Over-controlling with the stick and rudder is to be avoided. The slightest excess can be fatal when barreling along at over 400 mph just forty feet above the ground.

Of course, this is all happening on a kind of stage with up to eight competing racers rounding the pylons at once in front of over 50,000 paying spectators glued to the event from their vantage point of the grandstands and pit area. For the moment, the pilots must forget the audience and think only of the aircraft darting around them. They must keep their eyes swiveling to catch and retain in sight any competing planes that come close. The ideal is to keep an ongoing tab on those other planes, especially when banking around a pylon so as to lessen the possibility of a dreaded mid-air collision.

Encased in a bubble canopy, a greenhouse effect from the blazing sun causes the pilot to perspire profusely. In the turns, the G-force builds, pressing against the occupant in the cockpit, making him or her feel the course, either depleting the competitive spirit or prompting the pilot to try harder. Racing, after all, is not about

A pylon on the unlimited course at Reno reaches about forty feet into the alluring sky, where in a few moments the serenity of the wide open desert will be invaded by a horde of roaring fighter planes, scrambling for position out of the chute fresh from the air start. The magnificent and endless blue above beckons to the pilots. (1997)

the machine so much as the dedication and experience of the person doing the flying. The sound of the engine, its myriad parts clattering away, fills the cockpit and infiltrates the earphones built into the helmet. Fumes bellow from the exhaust stacks, mixing with the pervasive smells of burnt oil and human sweat. All of this occurs at hundreds of miles per hour only a wingspan above the buckskin earth in a metallic vessel being violently shaken by uneven air currents generated by the natural warming of the late afternoon.

Leveling the wings on the straightaway, the pilot may pour on the coals, accelerating to an even faster speed to gain precious seconds over others in the field. Approaching the finish, the decorated pylon abeam the center grandstand, the pilot yearns for victory as the ground rushes underneath. Throttle full open, willing the plane ahead of the others, the pilot, leans as far forward as the shoulder harness permits, until, off to the side, the flagman waves a checkered flag up and down in what is discerned as little more than a blur.

The race is won, but celebrating will have to wait, for the temperamental airplane must still be flown until returned to the ramp. At the end of the last lap, convention calls for pulling up high, gaining altitude quickly in case, after a grueling contest, the old warplane decides to poop out by throwing a piston rod or sucking in a valve. The winner climbs high, and the rest of the field follows.

Going Home Again: Past Glory

All glory is fleeting, but on occasion it may be recalled and savored. In 1999, the Reno air races began an annual ritual to formally recognize the best antique aircraft restorations. Joining with the Reno Air Racing Association, Rolls-Royce North America, the National Aviation Hall of Fame, and the Smithsonian Institution's National Air and Space Museum present a prestigious award honoring the airplane restoration that has been adjudged to be the most technically meritorious and historically accurate. For consideration, aircraft must be at least forty-five years old, airworthy, on site at the Reno air races, and not among the current crop of air racers.

How appropriate it was that the very first winner turned out to be an old air racer from Cleveland. Beating the fourteen other entries in the restoration contest, Bob Odegaard's F2G-1D Super Corsair, given its racing lineage, seemed ideally suited for the top honor. Odegaard, an aircraft restorer from Kindred, North Dakota, obtained the relic in 1995 and immediately began the monumental task of bringing the plane back to life. The restoration process involved more than 12,000 man-hours.

The Super Corsair, one of only ten ever built, had come off the assembly line in 1945 and never saw combat. It was sold off as surplus by the military in 1947. Two years later, with Ben McKillen at the controls, it finished third in the Thompson Trophy race. That year, 1949, represented the end of an era, for it was the last of the famous Cleveland air races. In subsequent years, the plane was housed at a variety of airports starting with race pilot Cook Cleland's airport in Willoughby, Ohio. After years of changing hands and languishing through inattention, the plane finally fell into Odegaard's care.

Resisting the temptation to turn the old racer into a Pacific war look-alike, Odegaard elected to restore the historic aircraft to its air-racing grandeur. Because the aircraft had deteriorated over time, many parts had to be fabricated from scratch. A Pratt & Whitney R-4360 engine, known as a corncob because of its double rows of fourteen cylinders, was located and installed to power the old racer. Despite the inevitable disappointments and delays in the meticulous rebuilding, number '57' rose into the sky again in time for the 1999 Reno air races. There were moments at Reno when spectators, unaware of the restored status of this Super Corsair, wondered why it was not competing in the unlimited heats.

The Rolls-Royce Aviation Heritage Trophy, sleekly sculpted and measuring four feet in height, was presented to Odegaard by a delegation of representatives from the various organizations sponsoring the award and special guest of honor at the Reno air races in 1999, former astronaut Jim Lovell. The ceremony took place on the ramp at the conclusion of the race weekend. By pre-arrangement, the trophy was at first put on display at the National Aviation Hall of Fame in Dayton, Ohio. When the new exhibit facility of the Smithsonian Institution's National Air and Space Museum opens at Dulles International Airport near Washington, D.C. in the centennial year of flight, 2003, the trophy will go on display there. In subsequent years, the trophy will alternate annually between the two institutions. Each year the winner will have his or her name engraved on a plaque at the base of the trophy.

In addition to the trophy, Odegaard won the 1999 People's Choice Award based on the preferences expressed by spectators at the Reno air races. Not only did the experts consider Odegaard's craftsmanship to be outstanding, the attendees were drawn to the old racer. Thanks to the Herculean labors of aircraft restorer Bob Odegaard, we got to see a resplendent plane fly again. And for those precious moments we were reminded of a past glory. The spirit of Cleveland came alive at Reno.

In 2000, the trophy and the popularity award went to another Corsair, the exquisitely detailed FG-1D in a standard wartime paint scheme, belonging to Ray and Sherri Dieckman of Corona Del Mar, California. The presentation was made by representatives from each of the sponsoring organizations as well as retired Air Force Brigadier General Paul Tibbets Jr, famous for piloting the *Enola Gay* on the Hiroshima mission. The awards appear to be fulfilling their objective of encouraging the preservation of aviation history through the restoration of antique airplanes to flyable status. Thus, the forward-looking Reno air races are destined to have an ongoing window, valuable and inspiring, into the past.

CHAPTER 2

Tangling Texans: The AT-6 Class

That old cliché that everyone loves a parade would enjoy nearly equal universality if the term 'air races' were substituted for the word 'parade'. There is something magic about big, heavy, boisterous radial-engine aircraft of an earlier era dashing across the desert at low levels, especially in multiple clusters. When the starter in the pace plane calls out those anticipated words 'Gentlemen, you have a race!', goose bumps form and eyes turn skyward.

At first, the line of approaching racers appears as if it might be a formation of old-fashioned advanced trainers on a mass instruction flight, a team of World War II cadets caught in a time warp.

But then, as the planes come nearer to the first pylon on the course, the airborne pack begins to scatter and it is clear that there is no formation. Moreover, the closer they get, the easier it is to discern varied paint schemes, more colors than the flavors at the local ice-cream parlor. Rounding that pylon and the others that follow, the AT-6/SNJ Texans, those durable 'Pilot Makers' of mid-century, fill the desert with an ear-splitting rumble that reverberates all the way down into one's innards. This is a portion of the 'heavy iron' at Reno.

AT-6s on the Ramp and in the Air

The reliable Pratt & Whitney R-1340 nine-cylinder radial engine contributed to the Texan's effectiveness as a training workhorse during World War II. The military view was that if you could master the Texan, you could fly practically anything then in the operational inventory. (*1998*)

Above: Occupying a parking space on the far west end of the pit area, *Lickety Split* shares ramp space with its crew van. In certain ways, air racing is getting increasingly sophisticated, with contestants' support vehicles sporting matching artwork, as here. *(2000)*

Above: Returning to the pit following an afternoon heat, veteran racing pilot Gene McNeely's number '90' is carefully pushed back to its designated parking spot. Ground safety has been admirable at Reno in part because the rules prohibit the starting of any aircraft engine until it is moved out of the pit and onto the roped-off ramp that adjoins the main taxiway. *(2000)*

The classic lines of the Texan are apparent on a late-afternoon stroll through the pit area. Here, Tom Martin's *Mis Stress* is about to be buttoned up for the night. (*2000*)

An entrant from British Columbia in Canada, this fire-engine red Harvard Mk IV, which belongs to airline pilot Keith McMann, can hardly be missed. Called the *Red Knight*, note the unusual star painted on the spinner. (*2000*)

Above: No opportunity is missed by the owners of air-racing aircraft to promote their cause. In the pit area, all kinds of mugs, dolls, clothing, and assorted trinkets are marketed by racing teams to defray costs and generate publicity. Here, the *Daring Diane* crew offers matching T-shirts next to the airplane. Of course, the plane's artwork has been accurately reproduced on the mementos which are for sale. (*2000*)

Above: Nicknamed *MY T6*, this aircraft's Navy markings belie the fact that it is a Harvard Mk IV. The Navy's designation for this advanced trainer type was SNJ. (*1999*)

Above: This breathtaking SNJ-5 carries the markings of a pre-war Navy aircraft: gray fuselage, yellow wings, blue tail surfaces, and a candy-stripe rudder. Note the red fuselage band and the diagonal red band stretching across the wing. Also, the famous Felix the Cat silhouette is painted on the fuselage. This plane is called, not surprisingly, *Felix.* It belongs to airline pilot Steve Dilda, whose wife, Mary, is also a pilot in the AT-6 Class. (*2000*)

Right: Rounding the pylons almost as if he were deliberately posing for the camera, Jim Good of Casper, Wyoming increases the angle of bank of the red, white, and blue *Wyoming Wildcatter.* Although finishing last in the 2000 AT-6 Class Gold race with an average speed of 217.548 mph, just qualifying for this level of the competition is a major accomplishment. (*2000*)

The two propeller blades of the AT-6 are short and, when turning at maximum revolutions, approach supersonic speed at their tips, which generates the distinctive thumping sound associated with the aircraft. Here, in what could pass for the beginning of a dive-bombing run, pilot Gene McNeely of Daytona Beach, Florida is on his way to a fourth-place finish in the 2000 Gold race with an average speed of 222.276 mph. (*2000*)

This semi-close-up shows Carter Clark of Capistrano Beach, California maneuvering his SNJ-6, *Daring Diane*, designated number '1'. Despite the aircraft's assigned racing number, it finished last in the 2000 Silver race, lumbering along at an average speed of 200.255 mph. (*2000*)

Among the most competitive air-racing pilots is Bakersfield, California cropduster Alfred Goss. His well-known solid blue SNJ-6, *Warlock*, regularly finishes within a few seconds of the Gold champion. Note the pilot's initials in block letters on the fin and rudder. (*1998*)

Another cropduster with the stick-and-rudder skills to prove it is Jerry McDonald of Tranquility, California. His plane's all-red paint scheme makes its nickname *Big Red* eminently appropriate. As can be seen, McDonald wears a matching flight suit. The bright white wing leading edges, which stand in sharp contrast to the surrounding blue, give the appearance of a heated razor slicing through butter. A long-time air-racing contestant, McDonald attained an average speed of 217.155 mph in the 2000 Silver race which resulted in a fourth-place finish. (*1999 and 2000*)

Left: This all-yellow Texan in U.S. Air Force markings is nicknamed *Slo Yeller*. It is flown by Dorel Graves Jr of Danville, Indiana. (*1997*)

Below: From this dramatic angle, the heart-pounding drama of rounding the pylons at full bore is immeasurable. Airline pilot Jim Booth of St Helena, California is at the controls as the sun's rays are momentarily reflected off the greenhouse canopy. (*2000*)

Right: An unusual paint scheme to say the least, this AT-6 is ensconced in World War II German camouflage. Nicknamed *Mystery Ship*, it was flown at the Reno air races by Van Nuys, California attorney Richard Sykes in 1997. (*1997*)

Below: As *Mis Stress* turns into the sun, its wing's leading edge glistens. Rare clouds float in the Reno sky and imposing mountains loom in the background. (*1996*)

Seen on a perfectly clear day, more the norm for Reno, *Mis Stress* looks like a different plane. Piloted by Tom Martin, the old trainer is captured in a moment of singular elegance. (*1999*)

Notwithstanding the 'New Orleans' markings on the tail, this trainer is piloted by Michael Gillian of Downers Grove, Illinois. Called *Big Easy*, the nickname for the City of New Orleans, the racing aircraft is noteworthy for the checkerboard detailing on the cowl's leading edge and on the tips of the fin and rudder. (*2000*)

Number '4' is called *Four Play*. The aircraft has red accents with yellow striping. It is piloted by well-known airman Lee Oman of Sequim, Washington. In the 2000 Silver race, he won first place with an average speed of 220.579 mph, which surpassed the performances of the fifth- and sixth-place finishers in the same year's Gold race. (*2000*)

In the skilled hands of retired airline pilot Bud Granley of Bellevue, Washington, *Lickety Split* put in a respectable performance in 2000, finishing fifth in the Silver race with an average speed of 214.715 mph. (*2000*)

Left: Robert Jones of Federal Way, Washington, a retired airline pilot like many of the contestants, flew his SNJ-6, known by the name of *Crossings Aviation*, to third place in the 2000 Silver race. His average speed was 217.610 mph. (*1999*)

Below: Nicknamed *Archimedes*, this Texan banks sharply as it approaches a pylon turn. It is piloted by Jim Eberhardt of Brea, California. (*1999*)

Big Wind, flown by airline pilot Carl Penner of Park City, Utah, is seen from contrasting angles: head-on with undulating mountains interrupting the horizon and banking steeply in a clear sky. The aircraft is unusual for an air racer in that, aside from its mandatory racing number and the almost obligatory American star and bars, it is virtually free of ornamentation. Penner captured the Bronze championship in 2000 with an average speed of 209.512 mph. (*2000 and 1996*)

The Gold champion in 1996 was Sherman Smoot, an airline pilot from Templeton, California, in *Bad Company*. This SNJ-6 won the race with an average speed of 221.677 mph. The all-black motif made this racer a standout. (*1996*)

Breaking out of the chute shortly after the start of the heat, the racers make a mad dash to establish their positions. It is at once colorful and breathless as the World War II era trainers reassert themselves in the desert sky. Note the barren backdrop and the pylon at lower left. (*1998*)

Giving the appearance of queuing as if by pre-arrangement, this line of five AT-6s is actually representative of competitive juices flowing at their max, each pilot balancing his or her craving for advantage with the need for safety. Importantly, this scene is not unduly hazardous, which is a tribute to the skill and professionalism of the contestants. (*2000*)

The sky over Reno fills with the rumble of radial engines when the racers are unleashed. Jockeying for position in a tight cluster as seen here, the competitors keep advancing until some wiggle their way from the pack, distancing themselves from the stragglers. (*1997*)

In a dogfight, *Archimedes* and *Red Knight* dueled throughout the 2000 Bronze race. While *Archimedes* inched ahead of *Red Knight* at the finish line, it had cut a pylon earlier in the contest. Accordingly, *Red* Knight ended up in third place with an average speed of 197.485 mph and *Archimedes* in fifth place with an average speed of 193.113 mph. (*2000*)

Seen here during the 1997 Reno air races, Steve Dilda in *Two of Hearts* and Jack Frost in *Frostbite* zip around one of the course pylons. That year, Dilda's wife, Mary, won the AT-6 Class Gold Championship in *Mystical Power*. The following year, Frost won in *Frostbite*. (*1997*)

Left: Longtime racers *Lickety Split* and *Tinker Toy* evoke the drama of closed-course air racing as their pilots, Bud Granley and Jim Bennett, respectively, turn up the power. (*1997*)

Below: Looking almost like the airplanes of cadets learning to fly formation, from left to right, Gene McNeely's number '90' (sometimes called *Undecided*), the Dildas' *Two of Hearts*, and the Eberhardts' *Archimedes* are really battling to pull ahead of each other. (*1998*)

Right: Tinker Toy tries to move up on *Crossings Aviation* in a scene that is typical of the AT-6 heats. Despite the frequency with which the races in this class have close finishes, they never get stale. In 2000, the elapsed time for the champion of the Gold race was approximately ten seconds under eight minutes. (*1998*)

Below: From another angle, the natural surroundings come into view. The sharp lines of the nearby mountains clearly define where the ground stops and the sky begins. The desert remains stoic, utterly oblivious to the feverish pursuit, the rampaging race planes eking out extra seconds where opportunity permits in their forward push. (*2000*)

Two formidable racers, banked at identical angles, turn the pylon in near unison. Gene McNeely and Jerry McDonald make air racing look easy. (*1999*)

Big Red and *Tinker Toy* joust in a perfect sky. As they try to edge each other out, the sandy surface of the desert floor reverberates with the thumping sound of the air racers. The lower they come, the louder their noise. (*1997*)

55

AT-6 Nose Art Gallery

Left: The nose art of Tom Martin's Texan is subject to interpretation. Could the nickname *Mis Stress* mean that the aircraft causes stress, or is the nose art supposed to infer that the aircraft serves as a kind of mate? Perhaps both perspectives are equally valid. Note the Pratt & Whitney emblem in the lower left. (*2000*)

Below: Nobility reigns on the flight line. The *Red Knight* is flown down from Canada by Keith McMann. It is noteworthy that the 't' is crossed with a knight's sword. Artistic details like this demonstrate the very personal imprint of the owners on their racing planes. (*2000*)

Right: Nose art in the tradition of World War II graces the side of Carter Clark's SNJ-6. During the war, it was popular for pilots to have an image of their wives, sweethearts, or pin-ups emblazoned on the noses of their planes. (*2000*)

Below: The white lettering stands out dramatically against the cherry-red coat of *Big Red*. Jerry McDonald's name also appears, though in much smaller script just below the canopy ledge. (*1999*)

Left: Nick Macy, a cropduster or, as some like to say, an ag pilot, is the proud owner of racing plane number '6', nicknamed *Six-Cat.* The Tulelake, California resident was the winner of the AT-6 Gold races in both 1999 and 2000. His aircraft is all-black except for the lettering and numbering. This nose art is located aft of the cowling and forward of the windscreen. (*1998*)

Left: Husband and wife Steve and Mary Dilda are both pilots who pursue flying with a passion. They have aptly named their plane *Two of Hearts*. Also, it has been assigned number '22'. (*1996*)

Below: Raced to a first-place finish in the AT-6 Gold Class in 1997 by Mary Dilda, *Mystical Power* is now piloted by Tom Campau of West Bloomfield, Michigan. In 2000, the aircraft came in second in the Gold race. Note the stylized thunderbolts under the magician's waving arm. (*1996*)

CHAPTER 3

Furious Fighters: The Unlimited Class

By absolute performance criteria, meaning attainable speeds and altitudes, they have long since been left in the dust because of superseding propulsion technologies. But the fighters of World War II vintage still retain their grip on the public imagination. For the sheer thrill of seeing 'heavy iron' in motion, all the jet blast in the world does not compare to a warplane of the 1940s, its largest moving parts in full view when streaming across the open sky in a low pass.

The unlimited racers are anachronistic because they are powered by engine types that are obsolete for everyday commercial air travel and air combat. They were built without the benefit of computer-aided design tools and their production configurations were conceived before many of the current crop of racing pilots were even born.

Yet, paradoxically, the racers that seriously contend for the Gold championship are viewed as cutting edge. The fastest racers at Reno have achieved world speed records for aircraft type. Indeed, many innovations have refined these old fighters, breathing new vitality into the proud designs originated a few generations ago. Aerodynamically streamlined cockpit canopies, clipped wings, advanced fuel injection systems, and many other modifications have all contributed to improving speeds as well as to raising expectations for the biggest, loudest, and fastest planes at the Reno air races.

Unlimiteds on the Ramp and in the Air

Row after row of fighters, like this North American P-51 Mustang, delight visitors to the pit. This is where crews prepare the mighty warplanes of yesteryear for a new kind of battle in the sky – the grueling speed contest that takes place in the form of laps around the 8.2688-mile unlimited course. (*2000*)

Left: Not all of the participating racing teams travel under austere conditions. Here, *Voodoo* is at the center of attention shielded from the sun by an elaborate tent as crew and invited guests enjoy the scene. (*2000*)

Below: The commemorative program booklet for the Reno air races in 2000 described *Voodoo*'s paint scheme simply as 'wild'. Like other Mustangs that have been highly modified such as *Strega* and *Dago Red*, this dramatically streamlined and power-boosted racer is considered a genuine contender for the Gold. (*2000*)

One of the all-time great unlimited racers, Bill 'Tiger' Destefani's *Strega* has fallen on hard times in recent years despite its designation as racer number '7'. Before a raft of technical problems arose, this aircraft racked up six Gold wins. Its familiar parking place in the pit is always shaded by a red tarp that matches the red of the plane's paint scheme. The added protection from the oppressive sun is welcomed by the dedicated ground crew that typically labors over the famous racer for hours at a time. It is hoped that the Bakersfield, California farmer who has thrilled air-racing audiences with sizzling finishes can overcome the nagging mechanical setbacks. (*2000 and 1999*)

The second-place finisher in the 2000 Unlimited Class Bronze race with an average speed of 365.781 mph was *Miracle Maker*, the P-51D piloted by Ike Enns of Tulsa, Oklahoma. The Mustang's naturally sleek design and majestic appearance reinforce the notion that there is elegance in simplicity. (*1997*)

The most patriotic color arrangement of any of the unlimited racers belongs to *Miss America*, the Mustang flown by Brent Hisey, a neurosurgeon from Oklahoma City, Oklahoma. After finishing second in the 2000 Silver race with an average speed of 427.535 mph, Hisey advanced to first place when the leader, Bill Rheinschild flying *Risky Business*, opted to move up to the Gold race. (*2000*)

Right: In the 2000 Silver race, *Risky Business* scored with an impressive average speed of 435.718 mph. However, when Bill Rheinschild elected to forfeit his Silver championship in order to compete in the Gold race, his average speed in the Gold race slipped by approximately 20 mph to 415.771 mph. This was still fast enough to garner third place. Near dusk, the last full beams of sunlight peek over the surrounding mountains in a virtually horizontal slant, signaling calm winds and quietude on the ordinarily bustling ramp. (*2000*)

Below: The P-51 that Robert R.A. 'Bob' Hoover used to fly stands out because of its all-yellow paint job. It is called, appropriately enough, *Ole Yeller.* Note the custom registration number below the horizontal stabilizer and elevator – the mandatory 'N' for all U.S.-registered airplanes followed by '51', the aircraft model number, and 'RH', the great air-show performer's initials. (*1998*)

Right: The unlimited races, given the spirited nature of the pylon heats, put such tremendous stress on engines that it is standard to see static run-ups adjacent to the pit area. Oil pressure and other engine values are checked ahead of a race as a safety precaution. Here, *Cottonmouth*, a camouflaged Mustang, runs the engine with brakes locked. (*1999*)

Below: Five-time Unlimited Class Gold champion *Rare Bear* preserved its dynasty until being toppled by *Strega*. Now both of the great racers are stricken with continuing mechanical difficulties. Sadly, *Rare Bear* has been grounded since its engine problems in 1997. Race fans hope that this superlative racing plane, a radically modified Bearcat, will find the necessary financial backing and return to the Reno sky. Its last Gold win occurred in 1994, when John Penny piloted it. In 1991, with owner Lyle Shelton at the controls, *Rare Bear* set the course record with an incredible average speed of 481.618 mph. (*1996*)

As its name implies, *Critical Mass* is a monster of an airplane. The heavily modified Hawker Sea Fury requires commensurate amounts of attention by its ground crew, who are charged with keeping the racer not only airworthy but competitive. Here, mechanics inspect the engine with cowl panels removed. (*2000*)

If ever there was a racer that exuded a sense of raw power from its looks alone, it would be the streamlined yet beefed up Sea Fury *Critical Mass*. Owned by Tom Dwelle, a retired Air Force fighter pilot and resident of Auburn, California, this exceptional plane sometimes starts slow but gains momentum. In the 2000 Gold race, *Critical Mass* finished second with an average speed of 434.962 mph. Actually, *Voodoo* was second to cross the finish line, but it had cut a pylon. The penalty allowed *Critical Mass* to advance a notch in the standings. (*1996 and 1997*)

Left: Michael Brown of Carson City, Nevada brought this stripped-down, all-aluminum Hawker Sea Fury to Reno in 2000. Reflecting the timing of the annual racing event and the aircraft's lineage, it is aptly named *September Fury*. (*2000*)

Below: This Sea Fury, called *Argonaut*, was flown by Brian Sanders of El Dorado Hills, California in the 2000 Unlimited Silver race. (*2000*)

Right: Another Sea Fury with a fitting name is the example flown by Art Vance of Sebastopol, California. Called *Furias*, this aircraft is a flying advertisement for its sponsor. The trend toward corporate underwriting of air racers is expected to continue, and possibly to expand. (*2000*)

Below: Winner of the Gold for three straight years, from 1998 to 2000, *Dago Red* is shown here taxiing to the active runway with Skip Holm of Calabasas, California at the controls. The aircraft also won in 1982. The other pilots were Bruce Lockwood and Ron Helve. Against the neutral earth tones of the rugged country-side surrounding Reno, the colors of *Dago Red* leap out at you. (*2000*)

The internationally recognized airman's hand signal, the positive thumbs up, communicates to the pilot, Jim Michaels of Dousman, Wisconsin, that he is cleared to flip the magnetos and start his engine. Note the propeller blades of this newly restored Hawker Sea Fury, *Miss Merced*, beginning to turn. (*2000*)

Miss Merced, recently out of the paint shop, would have won the award for most admiring glances at the 2000 Reno air races if such an honor existed. The ragged orange fingers stretching back from the exhaust stacks symbolize scorching flames, which suggest a very hot engine generating an extreme level of thrust. Note the aircraft's nickname painted on the landing gear door and the American flag emblazoned on the vertical stabilizer. (*2000*)

Left: Showing its stuff, *Miss Merced* goes into an extremely steep bank. The pilot, Jim Michaels, is a dentist. One wonders if he suggests this kind of flying as therapy for his patients. He won the 2000 Unlimited Bronze race handily with an average speed of 388.403 mph. The next closest challenger was nearly 23 mph behind. From this perspective out at the pylons, the dynamism of one of the sharpest-looking air racers can be appreciated. (*2000*)

Below: One of the 2000 Bronze competitors, *Sparky*, a fairly stock P-51, finished fifth with an average speed of 282.140 mph. Its pilot, Brant Seghetti, is from Vacaville, California. (*2000*)

Right: Looking almost like a combat-ready World War II or Korean War fighter, *Lady Jo*, a TF-51D, is another of the relatively stock Mustangs. Competing in the 2000 Bronze race, it recorded an average speed of 283.574 mph to finish in fourth place. The pilot was Rob Patterson of Corona, California. (*2000*)

Below: In 1999, the famed Bob Hoover's Mustang *Ole Yeller* was piloted in the Unlimited Class by its new owner, John Bagley of Rexburg, Idaho. Even though Hoover was not at the controls, it inspired people to see the recognizable fighter, still in Hoover's markings, rounding the pylons on the course at Reno. (*1999*)

The spectacular *Voodoo*, which not only looks amazing but is a real contender for the Gold, incurred a crushing penalty in the 2000 race for jumping the air start. Although the racer was the second plane to cross the finish line, it was knocked back to fifth place by air-racing officials because of the infraction at the start. Pilot Matt Jackson of Calabasas, California had one lap's time added to his total elapsed time. The addition of 64.43 seconds brought his total to nine minutes and 46.23 seconds, and as a result his average speed was reduced to 406.225 mph. *Voodoo*, seen here in knife-edge and furiously rounding a pylon, has great future potential. (*1999 and 2000*)

Similar in appearance to *Miracle Maker*, the Mustang *Ridge Runner* is piloted by Dan Martin of San Jose, California. The surrounding rugged terrain looms conspicuously in the distance as *Ridge Runner* approaches one of the course's eastern pylons in the late afternoon. As the aircraft gets closer, it becomes easier to ascertain the high rate of speed at which it is moving. In the 2000 Gold race, it was unable to complete the sixth lap, and therefore no racing speed was computed. (*2000 and 2000*)

Veteran air-racing pilot Jimmy Leeward, who operates the well-known and highly regarded pilot community the Leeward Air Ranch in Ocala, Florida, streaks past one of the pylons. Since Lefty Gardner's retirement, Leeward, a fantastic pilot, is considered the new king of pylon hugging. He brings his Mustang, *Cloud Dancer*, down to where you can almost reach out across the imaginary line connecting the pylons and feel the slipstream of the polished aluminum racer. In the 2000 Silver race, he came in sixth (or fifth, given winner Bill Rheinschild's decision to move up to the Gold), chalking up an average speed of 388.777 mph. (*1999*)

Air racing is fraught with danger. While it would be nice to enjoy immunity from disaster when speeding several hundred miles an hour at the equivalent of just a wingspan above ground, the reality is to the contrary. Pilots who compete at Reno are well aware of the hazards. Among them was longtime contestant Gary Levitz of furniture company fame. The Texas resident had flown an impressive array of racers during a career spanning nearly thirty years, including a P-38, a P-63, and a variety of P-51s. For three years, starting in 1997, he piloted an almost unbelievably souped-up Mustang, which he nicknamed *Miss Ashley II*. This racer incorporated many modifications such as Learjet wings, swept tail surfaces, and a Griffon engine turning contra-rotating propellers. Early in the 1999 Unlimited Gold race, as speed increased and as G-forces built up in steep turns around the pylons, the plane's elevators seemed to flutter violently, and then they and the horizontal stabilizers suddenly snapped off. The aircraft, already close to the ground, rolled uncontrollably and in moments it impacted the ground. Tragically, Levitz perished in the accident. His love of flight and his contributions to the sport of air racing will long be remembered. (*1998*)

Years before he tore up the sky in the elaborately redone *Miss Merced*, Jim Michaels piloted *Queen B*, a Mustang sporting a rather traditional motif. (*1997*)

When the Russian Yaks (for Yakovlev) first descended on the U.S. air-racing circuit in a major way around the time the Iron Curtain fell, there was speculation that these foreign types might give the old standard bearers a run for their money. Their small stature and sleek shape made it seem possible, but in practice that presumed scenario has not taken hold. This Yak, nicknamed *Czech Ride* and flown by retired airline pilot Sam Richardson of Aurora, Oregon, qualified for the 2000 Bronze race but was unable to finish the seventh lap. (*2000*)

Also sporting a red Russian star, this Yak, nicknamed *Maniyak*, is piloted by Tom Camp, a certified public accountant from San Francisco, California. Like the other Yak competing in the 2000 Reno air races, this one made the cut for the Bronze race. *Maniyak* finished third with an average speed of 343.777 mph. (*2000*)

Banking just enough to produce a glare off the starboard wing, *September Pops* commands attention for its stateliness. With Ione, California resident Randy Bailey at the controls, this lovely Sea Fury made it to third place in the 2000 Silver race (or second place when factoring in the winner's decision to advance to the Gold) with an average speed of 402.558 mph. (*1998*)

In one of those peculiar ironies, the Hawker Sea Fury nicknamed *Riff Raff* is piloted by one of the most distinguished aviators participating in the Reno air races. Robert 'Hoot' Gibson's logbook includes entries for pilot-in-command time on board the Space Shuttle. Eventually, Gibson, who had become a revered member of the astronaut corps, retired from the National Aeronautics and Space Administration. He had a remarkable flying career in the military and NASA. Upon leaving government service, he joined an airline where he accumulates even more flight hours as a Boeing 737 pilot. Even with his commercial flying commitment, it seems he pops up at about every other major U.S. air show at the controls of some exotic aircraft. If anyone is addicted to flying, it is Gibson. By the way, his wife, Dr Rhea Seddon, was an astronaut too. In 1999, the thirtieth anniversary year of the manned lunar landing, the Reno air races honored eight former astronauts including Gibson and Seddon. *(2000 and 1999)*

Although eligible for the 2000 Silver race, the newly painted *Furias* was not able to start. This image was captured earlier in the week as its pilot, Art Vance, was working through the matrix of competitions towards the final day of championship races. (*2000*)

The red kangaroo silhouette encircled by a blue roundel gives this Sea Fury a distinct south-of-the-Equator flavor, yet it is nicknamed *Spirit of Texas*. Not coincidentally, the racer is flown by airline pilot Stewart Dawson of McKinney, Texas. With an average speed of 392.580 mph, this racer finished sixth in the 2000 Unlimited Gold race. (*2000*)

Decked out in military colors, *Argonaut* made a credible showing in the 2000 Silver race with a fifth-place finish (or fourth place when the winner, *Risky Business*, was elevated to the Gold race) with an average speed of 389.298 mph. (*2000*)

The Sanders brothers, Brian and Dennis, are well-known aircraft restorers who are now linked to the formidable Sea Fury that carries the imposing nickname *Dreadnought*. In 1983, Neil Anderson flew the racer to a Gold championship. Again, in 1986, the silvery plane won with the late Rick Brickert at the controls. This image shows Dennis Sanders zooming past the clouds in the mammoth aircraft during the 1998 Reno air races. (*1998*)

Almost too fast to appreciate as a thing of beauty, *Dago Red* comes screaming at and then around the pylon. Wow! In the 2000 Unlimited Gold race, Skip Holm guided *Dago Red* to victory with an average speed of 462.007 mph. In 1998 and 1999, Bruce Lockwood piloted the racer to champion status with average speeds of 450.599 mph in 1998 and 472.332 mph in 1999. (*2000 and 2000*)

In a battle of the Hawker Sea Furies, Nelson Ezell in number '21' and Brian Sanders in *Argonaut* try to edge each other out in the 2000 Unlimited Silver race. Ezell finished a mere six seconds ahead of Sanders. (*2000*)

Over the years, the field of unlimited racers has been whittled down to just a few aircraft types, primarily Mustangs and Sea Furies. There are just not many Lightnings, King Cobras, Corsairs, or Bearcats remaining. Various influences account for this shortage, such as the levels at which certain types were consigned to the scrap yard after the war, parts availability, insurance affordability, etc. The decrease in racing types has not dampened enthusiasm, however, for the types that remain flyable are appearing at the races with an expanding set of airframe and color variations. The fresh modifications and new paint schemes seen on the course year after year help to keep interest strong in the sport of air racing. Here, in a 1996 unlimited race, Canadian Don Crowe is in the lead with his Sea Fury *Simply Magnificent* (note the maple leaf roundels) as Dennis Sanders, in number '281', trails close behind. (*1996*)

Left: Juxtaposing a vibrant airplane against a vibrant sky is liable to produce the effect seen here of *Dago Red* poised against Reno's crisp and clear, unblemished blue sky. The racer has been at it for years. The crowds have come and gone. In fact, so have the pilots. But the wind, the sky, the open vista, and the aircraft remain. *Dago Red* has seen it all and harbors a great many secrets. If only she could talk. (*2000*)

Below: This is not nose art at all. An innovation incorporated in the new paint job of this stunning Sea Fury was to place the nickname not on the aircraft's nose but on its landing-gear door. No lettering mars the decorative fuselage save for the compulsory air-racing number. (*2000*)

Above: A P-51 Mustang restored in the authentic World War II style, *Moonbeam McSwine* is a frequent sight not only at the Reno air races, but across the country at numerous warbird air shows. Vlado Lenoch of LaGrange, Illinois, noted for his flying prowess, revels in displaying his sparkling fighter. (*2000*)

Right: The exhaust stacks of the Merlin engine are the perfect prop (no pun intended) for the nose art on Brant Seghetti's P-51. The legendary engine developed by Rolls-Royce just in time to meet the demands of war was renowned for its reliability. To this day, the stock versions still hum synchronously, as if to say the skilled laborers who hand-made each engine knew more than half a century ago that their attention to detail in the assembly process might determine if the world got to live in freedom. Hopefully, that special sound and all that it represents will never be taken for granted. (*2000*)

Left: Logically, one could expect some pops upon the delivery of a couple of 500-pound bombs, even if delivered by helmeted storks flying formation as depicted in this whimsical nose art. Actually, this nose art is replicated from a B-24 bomber flying missions from England during World War II. The wives of both the bomber's pilot and co-pilot were expecting babies in September 1944. (*1999*)

Below: The red, white, and blue of *Miss America* are regular features every year at the Reno air races. (*2000*)

Right: Obviously, *Voodoo*'s paint job entailed minute detailing. Just imagine the care required to install the green striping and to ensure a uniform width. Note the safety plugs in the exhaust stacks and the dangling fabric reminder handle. (*2000*)

Below: Denver, Colorado attorney Joseph Thibodeau has been bringing his P-51 Mustang *Crusader* to the Reno air races for a number of years. The nose art includes not just the word, but an image of a mounted knight charging forward with banner in hand. The detail of the artwork is breathtaking. In a way, these elaborate paintings on the noses of old warplanes signify the equally meticulous attention to the working parts under the skin of the aircraft. (*1996*)

Left: Most of the nicknames turning up at Reno shun themes of belligerence. Instead, they tend to serve as an acknowledgement of a spouse or a play on words. Sometimes they are downright heartwarming and life-affirming, as depicted here in the nickname *Miracle Maker*. (*1996*)

Below: In 1996, airline pilot Robert Converse of Santa Paula, California brought this Mustang, *Huntress III*, to the Reno air races. Note the dagger form given to the letter 't'. Also in this close-up it is easy to see the construction materials and techniques of the generation before composite materials. Aluminum alloy, rivets, and traditional fasteners abound in the airframes of P-51s. (*1996*)

Right: There is no sign describing for the bystander the larger-than-life personality who used to tear up the sky over Reno in this P-51 Mustang, *Ole Yeller*. But then, many of those making their way through the aisles of the pit area already know of the great pilot who flew this plane. Old-timers can be seen to the side of the aircraft, arms outstretched around grandchildren, passing on the story. As ice-cream melts onto the tarmac and as the roar of current racers cracks the afternoon air, you know that the legend of Bob Hoover – combat pilot, test pilot, air-show pilot – lives on. (*2000*)

Below: Daylight begins to give way to night, but in the last glimmers of the waning sun the reflected beauty of the uncharacteristically quiet racing planes radiates a brilliance, both soothing and inspiring. It has been a good day, yes, even rewarding, and behind the impending dusk is another dawn. (*2000*)

CHAPTER 4

Winners' Circle

Reno tradition calls for the Unlimited Class Gold Champion to taxi up to the grandstands after winning the race. At the center of the ramp, and in front of tens of thousands of spectators, the victorious pilot is presented with the championship trophy in a short ceremony that is a concession to formality by an air-racing establishment that generally eschews the ornate.

In the middle of this scene are the winning pilot and his crew. Next are the air-racing officials and various presenters. Engulfing these participants is an army of photographers, pressing forward for that perfect camera angle for pictures to appear in the aviation magazines. A much larger crowd eventually filters down from the bleachers and swarms all over the champion, seeking autographs on programs and T-shirts.

The winning pilot typically accommodates all autograph requests, still wearing his fire-retardant flight suit even though he is probably soaked in sweat. There is an awareness that without all those fans clamoring for a moment of attention, these air races would not be happening. In time, all by itself the hubbub dissipates and the ground crew tows the newly ordained championship airplane to its normal parking spot in the pit. The pilot, by now winding down emotionally as both his adrenaline and his well-wishers recede, slips across the expansive ramp into the distance aboard, of all things, a golf cart.

Somehow in all this hoopla, the competing pilots who presented the greatest challenge poke through the layers of people to extend a congratulatory handshake to the winner, their fellow airman. The competition's intensity does not impair its sportsmanship. At Reno's hotels, casinos, and restaurants that night competing pilots and crew celebrate together. And the aircraft, bathed in darkness on the ramp, lie idle in a quiet decorum. These sparkling objects of inspiration, the nuclei of our dreams, we know, though dormant at this hour, will reawaken and stir our souls once again.

With barely enough time to catch his breath after winning the Unlimited Gold at the 2000 Reno air races, Skip Holm climbed back into the cockpit of *Dago Red* for the purpose of making a solo run in an attempt to become the first person to exceed 500 mph on the unlimited course.

Here, the crew chief and mechanics confer with Holm before he attempts to establish what would be a new course speed record. Unfortunately, as soon as he began the speed run he felt a shuddering; simultaneously his ground crew, which monitors performance parameters through an intricate telemetry system, reported a loss of oil pressure. It was no problem for the experienced pilot. He nursed his plane to one of the runways for an uneventful landing. Inspection revealed a badly mangled engine with a huge hole blown through the crank case. (*2000*)

As the ground crew makes its last round of inspections before the post-race record attempt, Skip Holm receives wishes of good luck from his family members in a final supportive gesture. The scene is reminiscent of Cleveland in the 1930s when Jimmy Doolittle won the cross-country Bendix Trophy race, but was not content to settle for that honor. During his stop in Cleveland, he refueled, kissed his wife, who handed him some sandwiches, and hurriedly departed for the East Coast to establish a new transcontinental speed record. From then to now the esprit has not changed; only the speeds have changed. (*2000*)

Left: The Unlimited Class Gold Champion in *Dago Red* for the two years prior to Skip Holm's win in 2000 was Bruce Lockwood. In the Winners' Circle, Lockwood receives the 1998 championship award on the wing of his racer. (*1998*)

Below: Another year and another triumph. In 1999, Bruce Lockwood shared a space on *Dago Red*'s wing with his ground crew. All smiles, champagne bottles uncorked, and the winning pilot raises two thumbs up, pointing to that nearly always inviting sky above Reno, Nevada. (*1999*)

Right: Not just the winner gets to occupy the ramp in the Winners' Circle. The top contenders, the planes that make the race a dead heat, get to join that special parking place at the conclusion of the Unlimited Gold race. Here, the impressive Hawker Sea Fury *Dreadnought*, a Gold winner in 1983 and 1986, is on display in front of the grandstands as spectators come down for a closer look. (*1998*)

Below: In 1997, the late Lloyd Hamilton flew *Furias*, a substantially modified Sea Fury, in the unlimited competition, and it, too, got to park before the crowd of aviation enthusiasts. Since then, the aircraft has been repainted. (*1997*)

Above: The ecstasy of glory was in evidence at Reno in 1997, the last year that Bill 'Tiger' Destefani won the Unlimited Class Gold Championship in his souped-up Mustang *Strega.* It is the custom for throngs of race fans to surround the winner, perhaps mirroring the phenomenon common at rock concerts and political conventions. Note the bent propeller blade tips. The damage was suffered in a minor landing accident immediately following the final race. (*1997*)

Left: Autographing mementos is a ritual at the Reno air races. An admirer gets Bill 'Tiger' Destefani to sign her T-shirt. Soon the ramp cleared and the sun set, leaving everyone from pilots to fans to contemplate next year at the Reno air races. (*1997*)

CHAPTER 5

Show Stoppers

The four-day event each September at Reno/Stead Airport is half air race, half air show. It just would not be feasible to launch different classes of racers one after the other without pausing in between. Some breathing space is needed between heats. Besides, after a while non-stop racing would get to be a bit tedious. Also, a lot of the attendees come with the expectation that the flying will be directly in front of them as they sit in the bleachers or stand nearby.

Accordingly, the event organizers have arranged the daily schedule to alternate continuously between air races and air-show acts. On occasion, a pilot doubles as an air-racing contestant and an air-show performer. For years, Lefty Gardner ruffled the sagebrush around the unlimited course in his Lockheed Lightning and then wowed the crowd with precision aerobatics in the same plane.

A younger generation of air-show pilots is using small, light planes designed expressly for precision aerobatics. These special aircraft are wrung out during the flying displays in maneuvers that include outside loops, flat spins, and repeated climbing torque rolls which are beyond the capabilities of most World War II era fighters. Yet the growl of the old warplanes grabs the air-show audience in a way that is unattainable by pure aerobatic aircraft. Demonstrating the popular bias toward warplanes, the crowd really takes notice and presses against the rope line when one of the military jet teams starts its routine.

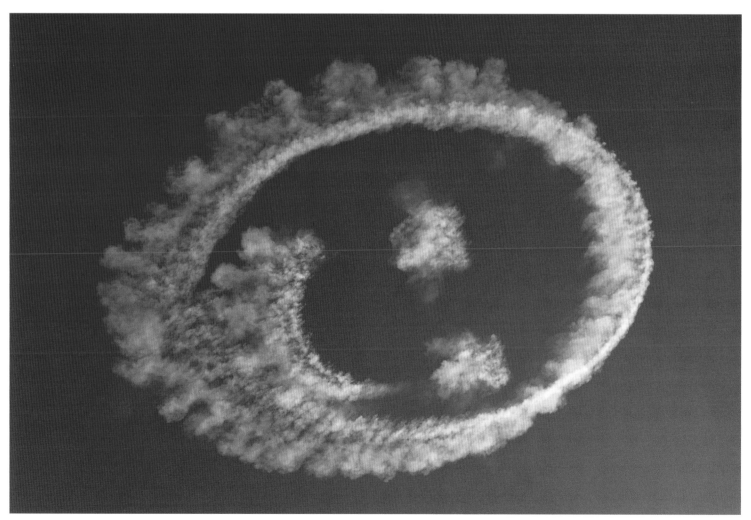

The dying art of skywriting is expertly demonstrated in the early-morning hours before any race gets underway. Steve Oliver and his wife, Suzanne Asbury-Oliver, paint the Reno sky with their creations formed by spurts of white smoke. What better way to greet arriving race fans than to present a smiling face in the sky? (*1998*)

Every day at the air races, the show is officially started with a parachutist unfurling the American flag as a rendition of the National Anthem is sung over the loudspeaker system. All activity on the ramp comes to a halt and all eyes focus on the waving flag as it slowly descends into the hands of a waiting ground crew at the center of the show line. (*1997*)

In 1998, former astronaut and Air Force fighter pilot Frank Borman showed up at Reno in his newly restored P-51, nicknamed *Su Su II*. He was not entered in the air races, but he did participate in some of the flybys, including a heritage formation flight with a currently operational F-15 Eagle. Note the absence of an air-racing number on the aircraft. (*1998*)

Nevada is a state laden with a military aviation presence, given its conducive flying environment and sparsely populated land mass. The naval air station at nearby Fallon usually sends a variety of its home-based and even some transient aircraft to the air races. This F/A-18 Hornet, with a top coat of desert camouflage that makes it blend in with the natural surroundings, thunders forward on take-off with afterburners lit. (*1998*)

The most often heard argument for why the military continues to field air demonstration teams like the Navy's Blue Angels, seen here, is that doing so helps recruitment. Of course, this is true, but an equally if not more compelling reason is that having such elite teams sets a standard. Moreover, if managed properly, everyone in the organization will strive for the same level of excellence, perhaps even seeking to be accepted as a member of the team. During the display depicted here, a youngster in the crowd at the air races asked her parents how the aviators of the Blue Angels do that, referring to their near perfect formation. The response was quick and to the point: practice, practice, and more practice. (*2000*)

Flying F/A-18 Hornet strike fighters, the superb airmen of the Navy's Blue Angels perform their signature maneuver – echelon parade – along the show line. No more than three feet from wingtip to wingman's canopy, these aerobatic flyers have to be sure not to hiccup. The team is home-based at the Pensacola, Florida naval air station and spends its winters training in southern California at the El Centro naval air facility. (*2000*)

Bursting out of a tight formation and corkscrewing through the open sky, the six performing team-mates of the Blue Angels demonstrate their talent for co-ordinated movement. At the same time, however, their seemingly effortless maneuvering into every corner of the sky evokes a profound sense of freedom, and elicits a yearning to be in the cockpit with them enjoying that opportunity to sail through the three-dimensional environment of the sky unshackled and unlimited. (*2000*)

For every take-off there must be a landing, and for naval aviators that is a complex proposition. Landing for these flyers means trapping one of four arresting wires laid across a sometimes heaving and pitching flight deck of an aircraft carrier that gives the appearance of a postage stamp in the middle of the ocean. Each Hornet here is configured for landing the Navy way – with tailhook extended. This formation is one of the few slow passes performed by the Blue Angels. During their comprehensive routine, the team exhibits the flight characteristics of the Hornet across a wide spectrum of the operational envelope, from slow to fast. (*2000*)

The Blue Angels need a support crew to follow wherever they go. Without the maintenance technicians and other staff, the team's jets would never get off the ground. In recognition of the invaluable contributions of these unheralded heroes, the transport plane that services the team is part of the flying display. Known as *Fat Albert*, the C-130 is operated by an all-Marine crew. In this image, the aircraft can be seen climbing out at a steep angle with the extra power of a jet-assisted take-off (JATO) system. Rockets are strapped onto the plane's belly and ignited to provide an extra boost when carrying a heavy load or departing a short runway. Here, of course, it is done just for show. Note the flame to starboard and the trail of dark smoke. (*2000*)

The Air Force air demonstration team, the Thunderbirds, has also performed at the Reno air races. Indeed, the team is stationed not far away in terms of jet fighter time, at Nellis Air Force Base near Las Vegas in southern Nevada. Seen here is one of the solo performers executing a roll during which the F-16 Falcon's underside is exposed. The silhouette of the mythical thunderbird from American Indian lore is the team's enduring symbol. According to legend, the thunderbird possesses great powers, including the ability to produce thunder. The F-16 is a highly maneuverable multi-role fighter. The pilots of the Thunderbirds are utterly exacting in their performances. *(1999)*

Not to be outdone, the air demonstration team from across the northern border – the Snowbirds of the Canadian Forces – operates indigenous side-by-side jet trainers. The CT-114 Tutor was designed in the 1960s as a primary trainer, and will continue to be used by the team for up to about five years into the new millennium. Unlike their North American counterparts, which operate six planes each in their flying displays, the Snowbirds fly nine aircraft in their routines. Here, the Snowbirds approach show center with landing lights and smoke on. (*1995*)

The nine-ship formations of the Snowbirds constitute an exercise in grace. Their pilots' adherence to precision is outstanding, as demonstrated in this breathtaking pass. The blue skies and generally warm temperatures of Reno are greatly appreciated by members of the Snowbirds since they are based in the less than hospitable climate of Moose Jaw, Saskatchewan. (*1995*)

Reno's Champions, 1964-2000

Unlimited Class

Year	Pilot	Aircraft	Speed (mph)
1964	Mira Slovak	#80 *Miss Smirnoff*	376.84
1965	Darryl Greenamyer	#1 *Greenamyer Bearcat*	375.10
1966	Darryl Greenamyer	#1 *Smirnoff*	396.22
1967	Darryl Greenamyer	#1 *Smirnoff*	392.62
1968	Darryl Greenamyer	#1 *Greenamyer Bearcat*	388.65
1969	Darryl Greenamyer	#1 *Conquest 1*	412.63
1970	Clay Lacy	#64 *Miss Van Nuys*	387.34
1971	Darryl Greenamyer	#1 *Conquest 1*	413.99
1972	Gunther Balz	#5 *Roto-Finish Special*	416.16
1973	Lyle Shelton	#77 *7¼% Special*	428.16
1974	Ken Burnstine	#33 *Miss Suzi Q*	381.48
1975	Lyle Shelton	#77 *Aircraft Cylinder Special*	429.92
1976	Marvin 'Lefty' Gardner	#25 *Thunderbird*	379.61
1977	Darryl Greenamyer	#5 *Red Baron*	430.70
1978	Steve Hinton	#5 *Red Baron*	415.46
1979	John Cocker	#6 *Sumthin' Else*	422.30
1980	Mac McClain	#69 *Jeannie*	433.01
1981	Skip Holm	#69 *Jeannie*	431.29
1982	Ron Helve	#4 *Dago Red*	405.09
1983	Neil Anderson	#8 *Dreadnought*	425.24
1984	Skip Holm	#84 *Stiletto*	437.621
1985	Steve Hinton	#1 *Super Corsair*	438.186
1986	Rick Brickert	#8 *Dreadnought*	434.488
1987	Bill 'Tiger' Destefani	#7 *Strega*	452.559
1988	Lyle Shelton	#77 *Rare Bear*	456.821
1989	Lyle Shelton	#77 *Rare Bear*	450.910
1990	Lyle Shelton	#77 *Rare Bear*	468.620
1991	Lyle Shelton	#77 *Rare Bear*	481.618
1992	Bill 'Tiger' Destefani	#7 *Strega*	450.835
1993	Bill 'Tiger' Destefani	#7 *Strega*	455.380
1994	John Penny	#77 *Rare Bear*	424.407 (Super Gold)
1995	Bill 'Tiger' Destefani	#7 *Strega*	469.029
1996	Bill 'Tiger' Destefani	#7 *Strega*	469.948
1997	Bill 'Tiger' Destefani	#7 *Strega*	453.130
1998	Bruce Lockwood	#4 *Dago Red*	450.599
1999	Bruce Lockwood	#4 *Dago Red*	472.332
2000	Skip Holm	#4 *Dago Red*	462.007

AT-6 Class

Year	Pilot	Aircraft	Speed (mph)
1968	Hendrick Otzen	#1 *Condor*	181.32
1969	Ben Hall	#7 *Miss Meridian Pavers*	190.90
1970	No AT-6 Class races were held this year.		
1971	Bob Mitchem	#94 *Miss Colorado*	205.85
1972	Mac McClain	#25 *Miss Eufaula*	201.59
1973	Bill Turnbull	#72 *Old Ironsides*	206.60
1974	Pat Palmer	#99 *Gotcha*	211.35
1975	Pat Palmer	#99 *Gotcha*	207.19
1976	Pat Palmer	#99 *Gotcha*	210.68
1977	Ralph Twombly	#41 *Spooled Up*	209.66
1978	Ralph Rina	#73 *Miss Everything*	205.71
1979	No AT-6 Class races were held this year.		
1980	No AT-6 Class races were held this year.		
1981	John Mosby	#44 *Miss Behavin'*	222.78
1982	Ralph Twombly	#44 *Miss Behavin'*	214.90
1983	Richard Sykes	#14 *The Mystery Ship*	225.94
1984	Ralph Rina	#73 *Miss Everything*	217.26
1985	Randi Difani	#18 *Thunderbolt*	213.89
1986	Eddie Van Fossen	#27 *Miss TNT*	223.450
1987	Eddie Van Fossen	#27 *Miss TNT*	226.362
1988	Eddie Van Fossen	#27 *Miss TNT*	229.759
1989	Tom Dwelle	#7 *Tinker Toy*	222.326
1990	Tom Dwelle	#7 *Tinker Toy*	229.264
1991	Eddie Van Fossen	#27 *Miss TNT*	227.028
1992	Eddie Van Fossen	#27 *Miss TNT*	234.766
1993	Eddie Van Fossen	#27 *Miss TNT*	226.885
1994	Eddie Van Fossen	#27 *Miss TNT*	224.704
1995	Charles Hutchins	#21 *Mystical Power*	231.430
1996	Sherman Smoot	#86 *Bad Company*	221.677
1997	Mary Dilda	#21 *Mystical Power*	228.003
1998	Jack Frost	#47 *Frostbite*	229.254
1999	Nick Macy	#6 *Six-Cat*	229.396
2000	Nick Macy	#6 *Six-Cat*	228.299

T-28 Class

Year	Pilot	Aircraft	Speed (mph)
1998	Rick Raesz	#29 *Monster*	273.017

Sport Class

Year	Pilot	Aircraft	Speed (mph)
1998	David Morss	#99 *Lancair IV*	308.184
1999	David Morss	#99 *Prototype*	319.671
2000	David Morss	#99 *Carbon Dreams*	328.045

Formula One Class

Year	Pilot	Aircraft	Speed (mph)
1964	Bob Porter	#14 *Little Gem*	193.44
1965	Bob Porter	#39 *Deerfly*	202.14
1966	Bill Flack	#92 *Rivets*	193.10
1967	Bill Flack	#92 *Rivets*	202.70
1968	Ray Cote	#16 *Shoestring*	214.61
1969	Ray Cote	#16 *Shoestring*	225.55
1970	Ray Cote	#16 *Shoestring*	220.07
1971	Ray Cote	#16 *Shoestring*	224.14
1972	Ray Cote	#16 *Shoestring*	223.95
1973	Ray Cote	#16 *Shoestring*	231.26
1974	Ray Cote	#16 *Shoestring*	235.42
1975	Ray Cote	#16 *Shoestring*	227.46
1976	Vince Deluca	#71 *Lil' Quickie*	228.75
1977	John Parker	#93 *Top Turkey*	226.12
1978	No Formula One Class Championship race held this year due to weather.		
1979	John Parker	#3 *Wild Turkey*	240.09
1980	John Parker	#3 *American Special*	249.07
1981	Ray Cote	#16 *Shoestring*	232.13
1982	Jon Sharp	#43 *Aero Magic*	224.52
1983	Chuck Wentworth	#69 *Flexi-Flyer*	239.02
1984	Ray Cote	#44 *Judy*	236.068
1985	Ray Cote	#44 *Judy*	229.09
1986	Jon Sharp	#43 *Aero Magic*	239.614
1987	Alan Preston	#44 *Sitting Duck*	232.989
1988	Alan Preston	#44 *Sitting Duck*	240.748
1989	Ray Cote	#4 *Alley Cat*	231.251
1990	James Miller	#14 *Pushy Cat*	237.405
1991	Jon Sharp	#3 *Nemesis*	245.264
1992	Jon Sharp	#3 *Nemesis*	238.175
1993	Jon Sharp	#3 *Nemesis*	246.849
1994	Jon Sharp	#3 *Nemesis*	248.911
1995	Jon Sharp	#3 *Nemesis*	249.904
1996	Jon Sharp	#3 *Nemesis*	238.950
1997	Jon Sharp	#3 *Nemesis*	245.043
1998	Jon Sharp	#3 *Nemesis*	245.257
1999	Jon Sharp	#3 *Nemesis*	243.513
2000	Ray Cote	#4 *Alley Cat*	245.912

Biplane Class

Year	Pilot	Aircraft	Speed (mph)
1964	Clyde Parsons	#11 *Parsons Twister*	144.57
1965	Bill Boland	#3 *Boland Mong*	148.68
1966	Chuck Wickliffe	#11 *Clark Dollar Special*	147.72
1967	Bill Boland	#3 *Boland Mong*	151.64
1968	Dallas Christian	#99 *Mongster*	175.13
1969	Dallas Christian	#99 *Mongster*	184.02
1970	Bill Boland	#3 *Boland Mong*	177.45
1971	Bill Boland	#3 *Prop Wash*	181.67
1972	Don Beck	#89 *Sorceress*	189.72
1973	Sid White	#1 *Sundancer*	194.95
1974	Sid White	#1 *Sundancer*	198.17
1975	Don Beck	#89 *Sorceress*	198.99
1976	Don Beck	#89 *Sorceress*	202.15
1977	No Biplane Class races were held this year.		
1978	No Biplane Class races were held this year.		
1979	No Biplane Class races were held this year.		
1980	Pat Hines	#1 *Sundancer*	206.62
1981	Pat Hines	#1 *Sundancer*	209.44
1982	Don Fairbanks	#5 *White Knight*	172.73 (Sport Division)
1982	Pat Hines	#1 *Sundancer*	209.40 (Racing Division)
1983	Don Fairbanks	#5 *White Knight*	179.59 (Sport Division)
1983	Pat Hines	#1 *Sundancer*	217.60 (Racing Division)
1984	Don Beck	#00 *Miss Lake Tahoe*	189.97
1985	Don Beck	#00 *Miss Lake Tahoe*	195.62
1986	Alan Preston	#00 *Miss Lake Tahoe*	192.665
1987	Tom Aberle	#31 *Long Gone Mong*	196.473
1988	Alan Preston	#00 *Top Cat*	205.918
1989	Tom Aberle	#40 *Wanna Play II*	196.140
1990	Danny Mortensen	#91 *Amsoil Pacific Flyer*	192.278
1991	Takehisa 'Ken' Ueno	#18 *Samurai*	195.273
1992	Jim Smith Jr	#88 *Glass Slipper*	193.893
1993	Patti Johnson-Nelson	#40 *Full Tilt Boogie*	208.466
1994	Earl Allen	#21 *Class Action*	203.311
1995	Patti Johnson-Nelson	#40 *Full Tilt Boogie*	202.124
1996	Patti Johnson-Nelson	#40 *Full Tilt Boogie*	212.811
1997	Earl Allen	#21 *Class Action*	198.736
1998	Jim Smith Jr	#88 *Glass Slipper*	201.599
1999	David Rose	#3 *Rags*	210.122
2000	David Rose	#3 *Rags*	209.434

Index of Aircraft Types

Author/photographer Philip Handleman, whose image is reflected in the shiny propeller blade of one of the racing Mustangs on the ramp at Reno, is not really working but having a wonderful time capturing subjects that inspire him. (*1999*)